THE IMPORTANCE OF

Elvis Presley

These and other titles are included in The Importance
Of biography series:

Alexander the Great	Adolf Hitler
Muhammad Ali	Harry Houdini
Louis Armstrong	Thomas Jefferson
James Baldwin	Mother Jones
Clara Barton	Chief Joseph
Napoleon Bonaparte	Malcolm X
Julius Caesar	Margaret Mead
Rachel Carson	Michelangelo
Charlie Chaplin	Wolfgang Amadeus Mozart
Cesar Chavez	John Muir
Winston Churchill	Sir Isaac Newton
Cleopatra	Richard Nixon
Christopher Columbus	Georgia O'Keeffe
Hernando Cortes	Louis Pasteur
Marie Curie	Pablo Picasso
Amelia Earhart	Elvis Presley
Thomas Edison	Jackie Robinson
Albert Einstein	Norman Rockwell
Duke Ellington	Anwar Sadat
Dian Fossey	Margaret Sanger
Benjamin Franklin	Oskar Schindler
Galileo Galilei	John Steinbeck
Emma Goldman	Jim Thorpe
Jane Goodall	Mark Twain
Martha Graham	Queen Victoria
Stephen Hawking	Pancho Villa
Jim Henson	H. G. Wells

THE IMPORTANCE OF

Elvis Presley

by
Adam Woog

Lucent Books, P.O. Box 289011, San Diego, CA 92198-9011

For Bill Ward, a good old Southern boy,
and for Kathy Kent Ward, who
once had a cat named Elvis.

Library of Congress Cataloging-in-Publication Data

Woog, Adam, 1953–
    The importance of Elvis Presley / by Adam Woog.
        p.   cm.—(The importance of)
    Includes bibliographical references and index.
    Summary: An account of the life of Elvis Presley and
his contribution to popular music.
    ISBN 1-56006-084-0 (alk. paper)
    1. Presley, Elvis, 1935–1977—Juvenile literature.
    2. Rock musicians—United States—Biography—Juvenile
literature.   [1. Presley, Elvis, 1935–1977.   2. Singers.]
    I. Title.   II. Series.
    ML3930.P73W65   1997
    782.42166'092—dc20   96–3955
    [B]   CIP
                                                              MN AC

Copyright 1997 by Lucent Books, Inc., P.O. Box 289011,
San Diego, California 92198-9011

Printed in the U.S.A.

Contents

Foreword

THE IMPORTANCE OF biography series deals with individuals who have made a unique contribution to history. The editors of the series have deliberately chosen to cast a wide net and include people from all fields of endeavor. Individuals from politics, music, art, literature, philosophy, science, sports, and religion are all represented. In addition, the editors did not restrict the series to individuals whose accomplishments have helped change the course of history. Of necessity, this criterion would have eliminated many whose contribution was great, though limited. Charles Darwin, for example, was responsible for radically altering the scientific view of the natural history of the world. His achievements continue to impact the study of science today. Others, such as Chief Joseph of the Nez Percé, played a pivotal role in the history of their own people. While Joseph's influence does not extend much beyond the Nez Percé, his nonviolent resistance to white expansion and his continuing role in protecting his tribe and his homeland remain an inspiration to all.

These biographies are more than factual chronicles. Each volume attempts to emphasize an individual's contributions both in his or her own time and for posterity. For example, the voyages of Christopher Columbus opened the way to European colonization of the New World. Unquestionably, his encounter with the New World brought monumental changes to both Europe and the Americas in his day. Today, however, the broader impact of Columbus's voyages is being critically scrutinized. *Christopher Columbus,* as well as every biography in The Importance Of series, includes and evaluates the most recent scholarship available on each subject.

Each author includes a wide variety of primary and secondary source quotations to document and substantiate his or her work. All quotes are footnoted to show readers exactly how and where biographers derive their information, as well as provide stepping stones to further research. These quotations enliven the text by giving readers eyewitness views of the life and times of each individual covered in The Importance Of series.

Finally, each volume is enhanced by photographs, bibliographies, chronologies, and comprehensive indexes. For both the casual reader and the student engaged in research, The Importance Of biographies will be a fascinating adventure into the lives of people who have helped shape humanity's past and present, and who will continue to shape its future.

IMPORTANT DATES IN THE LIFE OF ELVIS PRESLEY

1935

Born on January 8 in Tupelo, Mississippi.

1945

Wins second prize at the Mississippi-Alabama talent show for singing "Old Shep."

1948

Moves with his parents, Vernon and Gladys Presley, to Memphis, Tennessee. Enters L. C. Humes High School.

1953

Graduates from high school and begins work as a truck driver. Makes his first recording, for his own pleasure, at Memphis Recording Service, of two old tunes: "My Happiness" and "That's When Your Heartaches Begin."

1954

Hooks up with Sun Records producer Sam Phillips and musicians Scotty Moore and Bill Black. His first commercially released record, "That's All Right (Mama)," becomes a regional hit. Quits truck driving to concentrate on live performance.

1955

Begins management by Colonel Tom Parker, who arranges the sale of Presley's contract to RCA Records.

1956

Presley's first RCA single, "Heartbreak Hotel," becomes his first number-one hit. His first television appearances, on shows hosted by the Dorsey brothers, Steve Allen, and Ed Sullivan, cause a national uproar. The first Elvis movie, *Love Me Tender*, opens. His first long-playing album, *Elvis Presley*, becomes RCA's first million-selling LP.

1957

Purchases Graceland. Receives army draft notice in December.

1958

Inducted into army early in year. Mother dies in August.

1959

Meets Priscilla Beaulieu while stationed in West Germany.

1960

Released from the army. Releases his first post-army LP, *Elvis Is Back*.

1961

Performs in Hawaii, his last public appearance for eight years.

1967

Marries Priscilla Beaulieu. Records *How Great Thou Art*, a gospel album that wins him a Grammy.

1968

Daughter Lisa Marie is born. Scores a triumphant success with his Christmas television "comeback" special.

1969

The soundtrack LP of the TV special charts high and Presley's next single, "If I Can Dream," becomes his first million-selling record in three years. Completes his final feature film, *Change of Habit*, and decides to concentrate on live performance and recording.

1971

Performs nearly 150 shows in Las Vegas and Reno despite failing health. Receives a lifetime achievement award from NARAS. The street outside Graceland is renamed Elvis Presley Boulevard. Priscilla leaves Graceland and later files for divorce.

1973

Performs before an estimated 1.5 billion people on a program entitled *Elvis: Aloha from Hawaii by Satellite*. Divorce from Priscilla becomes final.

1977

Gives last performance in June. Dies at Graceland on August 16.

The King of Rock and Roll

Before Elvis, there was nothing.
> John Lennon

There have been contenders, but there is only one King.
> Bruce Springsteen

If you want to understand America, sooner or later you're going to have to deal with Elvis.
> writer Kevin Quain

A combination of talent and charisma made Elvis Presley the King of Rock and Roll. Elvis's radical style redefined American popular music.

There are other people named Elvis. There are even other singers named Elvis. For millions of people around the world, however, there is only one true Elvis. There is only one King of Rock and Roll.

For his entire adult life—from the time he was a teenager in the mid-fifties until his death in 1977—Elvis Presley was one of the most famous people in the world. In death he is even more famous. His records and movies continue to make millions of dollars every year, as do such items as books of photos: Elvis may have been the most photographed person in history, and it is said that his face has been reproduced more times than anyone else's. It is even rumored that he is still alive; Elvis sightings have become regular, even commonplace. It is as if Presley was so loved that some people cannot believe he was mortal, like any other human being.

There are several reasons for Presley's lasting fame. One involves his lavish lifestyle and troubled personal life. There are endless stories about his eating binges and drug addiction. There has been much talk about the women in his life and his failed marriage. Biographers have tried to analyze the reasons behind his eccentricities, such as his obsessive remodeling of Graceland, his gaudy mansion in Memphis. Much has been made of his dependence on the group of friends called the Memphis Mafia, the good old boys who devoted their lives to shielding the famous singer from the real world.

Stories about Presley's personal life often contain some truth. But these stories have grown over the years to ridiculous proportions. The commercial exploitation of Elvis—in music, movies, and every kind of marketable gimmick imaginable—only makes the details even more exaggerated.

The lurid aspects of the Elvis legend distract from his real and important role in shaping American popular music. Apart from all the juicy stories, Elvis Presley was an immensely gifted singer, who opened the floodgates for a revolution in popular music. With his records, in his performances, and in his life, he hit a nerve in American society; after his arrival, the world was never the same.

Elvis did not invent rock and roll. It can be argued that he was not even the music's greatest singer. But any history of rock will always lead back to him as a crucial source; he was, safe to say, the single most important person in its development.

His musical triumphs fell into three main categories. He was a great synthesizer, a great popularizer, and a great revolutionary.

The Myths About Elvis

In this excerpt from his book Elvis, *rock critic Dave Marsh reflects on the two basic myths surrounding Elvis.*

"No one myth is large enough to contain Elvis. . . . One contends that Elvis was a failure. He left Sam Phillips, Memphis and the South, Sun Records and rockabilly—his home and his place in the world—for Col. Tom Parker, Nashville, Las Vegas, New York and Hollywood, the Army, RCA Victor, a life of hookers, pills and dissolution. In this version, each step Elvis took was a descent, his career an arc of unrelieved disaster.

The second basic Elvis myth insists that he was a savior. . . . It is as if his fabled love made all the excuses necessary, not only for Presley but for everyone—as if the Elvis story were nothing but transcendence and triumph.

There's something foolish and mean about these extreme attitudes. . . . Let us concede the worst: that Elvis was nothing more than a junkie pervert. Let us grant the most outrageous fantasy: that he was a messiah, or, anyhow, a saint. So what? You don't need to be a great man to be a great artist."

His first great achievement was to *synthesize*. Working with his producers, who helped shape his sound, he brought together different but related styles to create a new type of music, one that had never been heard before. Before the phrase "rock and roll" caught on, this new stuff— a hybrid of country, gospel, blues, and rhythm and blues (or R&B) was called many names, including "cat music" and "rockabilly."

Elvis was also important because he *popularized* the music—that is, he made it accessible to a wide audience. At a time when racial tensions ran especially high, he introduced the passion and intensity of black music to a mostly white audience. In so doing, he showed respect for black music, helped break down racial barriers, and paved the way for artists of all races to succeed.

Finally, Elvis *revolutionized* youth culture and became the symbol for his rebellious generation. He combined the sexy, dangerous aspects of rock with the image of a wholesome Southern boy who always had perfect manners and a sweet smile. He was a charmer, but he was also a powerful, earthy presence in an era of bland, dull pop music. Parents hated him, kids loved him. Whether loved or hated, he could not be ignored.

Things changed as he got older. His canny manager, Colonel Tom Parker, steered him into middle-of-the-road movies and music that made him acceptable even to nervous adults. Over the years, though, the excesses of his personal life began to take their toll; by the end, overweight and disoriented from drug abuse, he had become a bloated parody of himself. He was a recluse, cut off from reality and from the fans who loved him. Always subject to dark,

Throngs of fans surround the stage as Elvis performs. His music and performances attracted many young people and helped to revolutionize youth culture during the 1950s.

moody depressions, he never fully recovered from the emotional nosedive that followed the collapse of his marriage. Even as he was at the top professionally, entertaining over a billion people with a groundbreaking worldwide satellite concert, he remained a strange, lonely figure.

Elvis Presley was a fascinating puzzle, a man of many contradictions. He was cool and uncool. He was sexy and sweet. He was a poor boy who triumphed over impossible odds and a sad lesson in the dangers of success. He was a genius who created a fantasy world for himself and a tragic figure trapped in a life he could not escape. He was Elvis.

1 The Early Years

Elvis was an old redneck boy who loved gospel and drove a truck. He might just about as well have grown up to be [TV evangelist] Jerry Falwell. For a boy with Elvis's background to move the way he did suddenly proved something.

writer and Southerner
Roy Blount Jr.

Tupelo is a tiny farming community in the northeast corner of Mississippi. In the thirties, when Elvis Presley's story begins, Tupelo was suffering, along with the rest of the country, from the economic disaster of the Great Depression. It was a poor town, and East Tupelo, where Elvis was born, was one of its poorest neighborhoods.

The Presleys and the Smiths, both poor farming families, had been in the area for generations when Vernon Elvis Presley and Gladys Love Smith married in June 1933. He was seventeen and she was twenty-one. They had to borrow from friends to come up with the three-dollar fee for the wedding license.

At first, they lived with their families. Vernon worked with his father harvesting cotton, corn, and peas. After two years of marriage, the couple moved into a place of their own; Vernon found work driving a milk truck and Gladys had a job as a sewing-machine operator at the Tupelo Garment Company. They worked long hours, Monday through Saturday, and considered themselves lucky if between them they made twenty-five dollars a week—but they were surviving.

The Birth

When Gladys became pregnant in the summer of 1934, she quit her job. The pregnancy was difficult and she could not work. That same year, the Presleys moved to a new house on Old Saltillo Road that Vernon had built with his brother and his father on property owned by Vernon's boss, Orville Bean.

It was a two-room shack, typically known as a shotgun house because buckshot fired through the front door would go straight out the back door. The entire house measured only thirty feet by fifteen feet. The front bedroom had enough space for an iron bedstead and a dresser, and the kitchen–dining room behind it had a table and a stove. There was electricity but no running water; in the dirt yard out back were a water pump and an outhouse, along with chickens and a cow.

(Left) The meager two-room house in Tupelo, Mississippi, where Elvis Presley was born on January 8, 1935. (Below) Elvis Aron, the only son of Vernon and Gladys Presley, was showered with love and attention during his childhood.

It wasn't much, but it was home, and Elvis Aron Presley was born there on January 8, 1935. The doctor's delivery fee, fifteen dollars, was paid by welfare.

The baby was given his father's middle name. Although unusual, "Elvis" was not completely unheard-of in the South in those days. It is a variation on an ancient Scandinavian name, Alviss, meaning "all-wise." His middle name—spelled with one "A" on the birth certificate—comes from the Bible.

Elvis was the second of twins, born about half an hour after his brother, Jesse Garon, who had been delivered still-born—that is, dead at birth. While the mother and the surviving baby rested, Jesse Garon was laid out in a little coffin, then buried the next day in an unmarked grave. All his life, Elvis was fascinated and terrified by the thought that he had possessed and then lost a double.

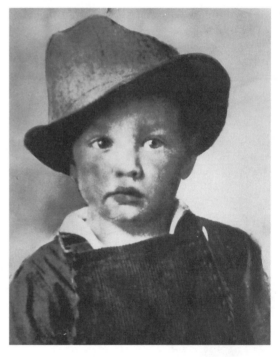

A Protected Childhood

Perhaps especially because his twin did not live, Elvis was treated with particular care by his parents. All his life, he would be given everything the Presleys could afford to give him. He was taught proper Southern manners—he always called his elders "Sir" or "Ma'am" and always stood to greet them—but he also learned that rules that applied to most people did not apply to him. As biographer Howard

DeWitt put it, "Vernon and Gladys believed that Elvis was a 'special creation' sent by the Lord, and they speculated that he had a special destiny."[1]

Gladys rarely worked during Elvis's childhood, so he grew up with her full attention. Even their neighbors—who also had the Southern tradition of cherishing family—found the closeness between Gladys and Elvis strange. Faye Harris, a neighbor, recalled, "She worshiped that child from the day he was borned to the day she died."[2] Elvis was always unusually close to his mother. All her life, they called each other by pet names and spoke in baby talk. As Elvis's Uncle Vester once put it, "He was a quiet, obedient boy who lived to please his mother."[3]

The Presleys were poor, and the family was on welfare from time to time. Vernon's work was unsteady and badly paid, and he was not ambitious about finding jobs in the first place. An impractical but charming dreamer, Vernon was "like a beautiful baby and Gladys was his mother,"[4] according to Elvis's childhood friend Jim Denson. Still, the family was tightly knit and extremely loyal to each other.

In 1937 Vernon was caught trying to alter the amount of a check given to him in payment for a hog. The crime was more an act of depression-era desperation than of real crookedness, but Vernon served eight months of a three-year forgery sentence. His wife and child visited him every weekend; Gladys found occasional factory work and moved in with various family members in the meantime. In 1940 the family moved briefly to Biloxi, Mississippi, where Vernon found work in the shipyards. During World War II, he moved to

"We Never Put Anybody Down"

Elvis grew up with dignity, despite such terrible poverty that the most a man could hope for was to stay out of jail. Vernon Presley elaborates on those hard times in this quote from Peter Guralnick's Last Train to Memphis.

"'I told Elvis,' said Vernon, 'that I'd work for him and buy him everything I could afford. If he had problems, he could come to me and I'd try to understand. I also said, "But, son, if you see anything wrong going on, promise me you'll have no part of it. Just don't let anything happen so that I'd have to talk to you between [prison] bars. That's the only thing that would break my heart."'

'There were times we had nothing to eat but corn bread and water,' recalled Vernon not long before he died, 'but we always had compassion for people. Poor we were, I'll never deny that. But trash we weren't. . . . We never had any prejudice. We never put anybody down. Neither did Elvis.'"

Memphis to work in a munitions factory and came home only on weekends.

Elvis started school in 1941 at East Tupelo Consolidated School. Gladys walked the mile-long trip with her son every day. He was an undistinguished student: polite, quiet, not good at academics but not bad either. In the words of his fifth-grade homeroom teacher, Mrs. J. C. Grimes: "Sweet, that's the word. And average. Sweet and average."[5]

In the fall of 1946 he transferred to Milam Junior High. It was there that "sweet and average" Elvis Presley would begin to show signs that he was very special indeed—and all because of a present he received on his eleventh birthday.

First Glimmer of Music

According to some stories, the birthday boy had asked for a bicycle; according to others, a rifle. In any event, he did not get what he wanted. Gladys bought Elvis a little guitar for $12.95 at a hardware store. It was cheaper than either a bicycle or a gun. Even though it wasn't his heart's desire, Elvis liked the new present. Vernon's brother, Elvis's Uncle Vester, taught the boy a few simple chords, and he began picking out songs.

These first fumblings with a guitar were not his only exposure to music, or even to public singing. The year before, he had stood on a chair and sung a sentimental ballad, "Old Shep," in a talent contest at the Mississippi-Alabama Fair and Dairy Show. He'd won second prize: five dollars and free admission to all the rides.

Elvis grew up listening to all sorts of music. As critic Dave Marsh has com-

A young Elvis poses for a portrait with his parents, Vernon and Gladys. Elvis and Gladys had an unusually close relationship and often called each other by pet names.

mented, a wide variety of sounds—radio and live performance, church hymns and pop music, white country and black blues—were important influences on Presley: "Music was in the air all around him."[6]

Radio was the Presleys' chief form of entertainment, and Elvis soaked it up. He enjoyed country stars like Hank Williams and Jimmie Rodgers, and he listened closely to pop crooners like Bing Crosby, Frank Sinatra, and Dean Martin. He also occasionally heard black R&B and blues, or "race music" as it was known.

Most important of all, Elvis also grew up with church music. His deeply religious

Elvis's childhood was strongly influenced by music, including gospel, country, and blues. He was introduced to the guitar in 1946, when he was given one as a gift for his eleventh birthday.

The gospel quartets—four singers, usually male—that Elvis heard in church were his deepest and strongest musical influences. These quartets sang either a capella (without instruments) or with minimal accompaniment, a single guitar or piano. Elvis especially loved the dramatic style of Jake Hess, the lead singer of the Statesmen Quartet; Hess, in turn, was heavily influenced by the soulful harmonies of black gospel singing. Like the Pentecostalist preachers, he could whip congregations to a fever pitch.

Singing at School

Elvis grew more determined with his music as he got older. In the seventh grade, he started taking his guitar to school. He would get together at lunchtime with a classmate named Billy Welch to play and sing. They liked current popular songs and white gospel tunes, as well as hillbilly music (as bluegrass and country tunes were then called).

Elvis was already beginning to dream of fame. According to another classmate, Roland Tindall, Elvis told anyone who would listen that he was going to be a star someday. Referring to a famous country-music radio show, Tindall recalled, "He told us he was going to be on the Grand Ole Opry. Not bragging; he just made the statement."[8]

Not everyone looked kindly on Elvis's singing. Often, he was ridiculed by teachers and classmates as a trashy boy playing uncouth hillbilly music. At the beginning of the eighth grade, a gang of boys even took Elvis's guitar away from him and cut the strings. Other classmates chipped in, however, and bought him a new set.

parents attended the First Assembly of God Church, which practiced a form of fundamentalist Christianity called Pentecostalism. The services were sometimes wild and ecstatic, with the ministers "speaking in tongues"—that is, saying words in unknown languages—when moved by the Holy Spirit. For this reason, Pentecostalists were known by many as Holy Rollers, a term Elvis disliked all his life.

The First Assembly of God did not have a separate choir, but Elvis and his family sang hymns along with the rest of the congregation. Church was a welcome refuge from the grimness of life in Tupelo, and Elvis sometimes went there to think in private about his problems. Years later, he recalled, "When I was four or five, all I looked forward to was Sundays, when we all could go to church. This was the only singing training I ever had."[7]

Then, in November 1948, Elvis attended his last day of school in Tupelo. At the request of his teacher, who liked to encourage the shy boy to sing, he gave the class a little concert as a going-away present. The next day, the Presley family moved across the state line to Memphis, Tennessee. They were in search of a better life.

A New City

The move to Memphis was motivated by simple economics: jobs were better there. "We were broke, man, broke, and we left Tupelo overnight," Elvis said years later. "Dad packed all our belongings in boxes and put them on the top and in the trunk of a 1939 Plymouth. . . . Things had to be better."[9]

Memphis had about three hundred thousand people, making it Tennessee's largest city. It was quite a switch from sleepy Tupelo, where the family at least had lived in their own home. In Memphis, their first residence was one room of a rundown house. They shared a bathroom with three other families, and Gladys prepared meals over a hot plate because there was no kitchen.

Vernon found work driving a grocery truck, then at a paint company and a tool factory. Gladys found occasional work as well, in a curtain factory or as a waitress. Elvis entered L. C. Humes High School.

The Presleys were also accepted at Lauderdale Courts, a low-income housing project. Their apartment at 185 Winchester Street was in a pleasant, eleven-year-old brick building. They had two bedrooms, a living room, a kitchen, and a private bath.

Southernness

In this excerpt from Elvis, Or the Ironies of a Southern Identity, *an essay reprinted in* The Elvis Reader, *sociologist (and Southerner) Linda Ray Pratt comments on how Presley kept his essential Southernness.*

"At the very moment in which Southerners proclaim most vehemently [strongly] the specialness of Elvis, the greatness of his success, they understand it to mean that no Southern success story can ever be sufficient to satisfy a suspicious America.

Elvis was truly different, in all those tacky Southern ways one is supposed to rise above with money and sophistication. He was a pork chop and brown gravy man. He liked peanut butter and banana sandwiches. He had too many cars, and they were too pink. He liked guns, and capes, and a Venus de Milo water fountain in the entry at Graceland. . . . His taste never improved, and he never recanted anything. He was the sharecropper's son in the big house, and it always showed."

It was close to Vernon's work and only ten blocks from Elvis's school. It was the best home they'd ever had.

Humes

Humes High must have been frightening for Elvis at first. It had sixteen hundred students—more people than in all of East Tupelo. Most of the kids came from poor white families like the Presleys. But Elvis was new, and he was strange—shy and awkward, with a thick country accent and a sensitive nature.

He also had unusual looks; in photos of the time, his heavily lidded eyes are dark rimmed, sleepy, and vaguely dangerous. His teachers, though, remember him as serious, quiet, and polite. "He was a gentle, obedient boy," remembered his ninth-grade homeroom teacher. "His English was atrocious . . . but he had a warm and sunny quality about him which made people respond." His twelfth-grade history teacher recalled, "At times he seemed to feel more at ease with [the teachers] than with his fellow students."[10]

Academically, he was average. He did poorly in music, probably because the kind of music taught in school bored him. Gradually, though, he began to assert himself. When a music teacher told him he couldn't sing, he replied politely that he could, but she just didn't appreciate his style. The next day, he brought his guitar to class and sang "Keep Them Icy Cold Fingers Off of Me," a recent country hit, in an attempt to prove his point.

When the school day was over, Elvis loved to play football. Though too small to be a star, he was feisty, and he played for the Humes High Tigers during his junior year. He liked metal and wood shop, and began thinking about becoming an auto mechanic after graduation. He also volunteered at a local library and joined ROTC,

A yearbook page from L. C. Humes High School shows a teenaged Elvis with heavily lidded and dark-rimmed eyes. The inscription next to his name reads "Best luck to a swell guy. Elvis."

Elvis's weirdness in high school, says Dave Marsh in Elvis, *was no put-on.*

"He seized every opportunity to express himself: football, the gospel sings, sharp clothes and long hair. Elvis didn't dress strangely to *become* weird; he chose flashy outsider's clothes because he *was* weird. Set down in the poorest section of Memphis at the crucial age of thirteen, he moved from a world of fewer than 10,000 people, where everyone at least knew *about* everyone else, to a world of more than 300,000 that couldn't have cared less about a poor cracker kid—that gaped at his hick idea of what was suave when it paid attention at all."

the Reserve Officers' Training Corps program of the U.S. Army.

More Music

Gradually, Elvis's playing and singing improved. Gladys asked Jessie Lee Denson, the son of the Presleys' preacher, to show her son a few things on the guitar. Jessie Lee, two years older than Elvis and something of a wild boy, gave him weekly lessons in the housing project's laundry room, the only private place they could find.

Elvis also got together with other boys who lived at Lauderdale Courts to practice their harmony vocals. They liked to hang around outside the project, singing in the warm Memphis evenings as other residents called out requests. Such evenings were just for fun, with no thought to singing professionally. And although Elvis liked to play at parties, he was still shy about singing by himself in public. Sometimes, he would ask for all the lights to be turned out before he would sing.

Elvis started work as soon as he could. He worked during the summers as a yard boy. He also got part-time work during the school year as a movie-theater usher: five hours nightly, $12.75 a week. As writer Howard DeWitt put it, "There was a definite blue-collar, working-class side to Elvis Presley's personality. . . . Elvis often bragged to his friends that work was more important than high school. In private, however, Elvis confided to other friends that he also loved school."[11]

In 1950, Vernon hurt his back and the family was faced with medical bills, and the need for Elvis to earn money became greater. For a time, while still in school, Elvis was on the assembly lines at Precision Tool and at Marl Metal Products. He worked from 3:00 in the afternoon until 11:30 at night. When he began to fall asleep in class, however, his parents made him quit; instead, Gladys went to work as a nurse's aide at St. Joseph's Hospital.

During his junior year, though he remained gentle and well mannered, Elvis's appearance and tastes began to change. He grew his sideburns and hair outrageously long. He greased back his DA ("duck's ass") haircut, which in later years he always said was in imitation of hairstyles favored by truck drivers. When he refused to cut his hair, the Humes High football coach kicked him off the team.

Elvis also became a snappy dresser. He favored flamboyant shirts, pleated trousers, and wild sports coats from a menswear shop called Lansky Brothers. This store was just off Beale Street, the legendary home of the blues and a focal point of Memphis's black community. The patrons at Lansky Brothers were mostly black; for Elvis to shop there, considering the times, was radical and daring.

And Elvis became firmly hooked on black music. He had seen a little African-American culture before he moved to Memphis, but the city was his first serious exposure to it. The richly expressive music struck a responsive chord in his developing personality. As Howard DeWitt noted, "For Elvis, listening to Billy Ward and the Dominoes, Ike Turner's Kings of Rhythm, and Sonny Til and the Orioles was simply an aspect of his education and his maturation."[12]

He still enjoyed white gospel, like the daily *High Noon Roundup* program on station WMPS, but the vivid sounds of R&B and the blues really grabbed him. Radio station WDIA, a black-owned station, featured disc jockeys B. B. King and Rufus Thomas, who themselves later became famous musicians. Over on white-oriented WHBQ, a jockey named Dewey Phillips had his own popular blues show.

Elvis loved to cruise the streets at night in his father's 1941 Lincoln and listen on the car radio to records by artists like Arthur "Big Boy" Crudup, Wynonie Harris, and Lloyd Price. He also attended whites-only Sunday-night shows at a local black theater, where he could hear both hometown artists such as Bobby "Blue" Bland and visiting stars like Fats Domino.

Graduation

Early in 1953, during Elvis's senior year, the Presleys moved to the downstairs half of a house at 398 Cypress Street. Because

During high school Elvis became a snappy dresser, wearing pleated trousers and wild sports coats. Once he became an entertainer, this flamboyant style became his trademark.

Black and White

Dave Marsh comments in Elvis *on the occasional intermingling of white and black cultures of the South in the 1930s. "Pegged" pants were baggy at the waist and extremely tight at the ankles.*

"Elvis' interest in black gospel music violated no cultural taboo. More than a few whites attended the black gospel shows in Memphis. . . . Still, it was fairly unusual for a teenager to be so caught up in gospel singing and to dress as eccentrically as Elvis did. Few other kids at the gospel sings wore pink pegged slacks; the other kids with DA haircuts hardly went to church. . . . This was a reflection on the contradiction that would plague Elvis his whole life: On the one hand, he had a tremendous wish to join the crowd; on the other, an equally powerful need to *show 'em*."

of Gladys's job, they were no longer eligible for low-income housing. Their upstairs neighbors were a rabbi and his wife, and the families became friendly. Elvis did household chores for the Jewish couple during the one day of each week, the Sabbath, when Orthodox Jews cannot work. In return, the rabbi and his wife let the Presleys use their telephone.

In April Elvis performed at his school's annual talent show. Listed sixteenth on a bill of twenty-two performers was "Elvis Prestly." There were so many performers that the only encore allowed was by the one who received the most applause: Elvis. That spring, he also attended the senior prom. His date was Regis Vaughan, a former neighbor at Lauderdale Courts. She could not convince Elvis to dance, however; he claimed at first that he was too shy and then admitted that he didn't know how.

Elvis graduated on June 3. In the Humes High yearbook for 1953, under a picture of Elvis, a caption explains that he majored in shop, history, and English. His activities included ROTC and four clubs: biology, English, history, and speech. Music was still just a hobby, and Elvis seemed to be destined for a workingman's life like his father's. Even before graduation, he'd arranged for his first full-time job, as a factory worker at M. B. Parker Machinists' Shop.

Elvis soon quit Parker for a similar position at Precision Tool, then left that one to become a truck driver for the Crown Electric Company. He was one of two drivers employed by Crown to take supplies to electricians on job sites. The pay was better—he was now getting $1.25 an hour. Plus, he got to drive a truck, which beat working in a factory. It was the last blue-collar job he ever held.

2 The First Recordings

He was like a mirror in a way; whatever you were looking for, you were going to find in him.

Marion Keisker of Memphis
Recording Service

If Elvis Presley's life story means anything at all, it means speaking to the heart of the human desire for freedom and liberation, from the feet to the hips to the heart to the brain.

writer Dave Marsh

Shortly after graduation, Elvis thought he had enough experience to give professional singing a shot. He wanted to join a gospel quartet, so he started pressing for a chance to perform at the regular "sings" he had been attending. Among his favorite groups was the Blackwood Brothers, celebrities on the gospel circuit and regulars on the WMPS show *High Noon Roundup.* James Blackwood recalled that in those early days Elvis was always hanging around, waiting for a chance: "Elvis liked to sing, you could see that. Singing came natural to Elvis, all right."[13]

When an opening appeared with a local quartet called the Songfellows, Elvis asked for an audition. Unfortunately, the Songfellows member who was going to quit changed his mind and the opening disappeared.

Shortly afterward, Elvis got another chance—this time with a club band. Eddie Bond, a veteran Memphis performer, needed a new singer for his group, and Elvis auditioned one night at a local joint called the Hi Hat Club. He sang a couple of numbers with Bond's band onstage, but he didn't impress Bond and didn't get the job. Bond claimed in later years that he was the only person who ever fired Elvis Presley from the bandstand.

Elvis took the rejections hard and was depressed for weeks. He was also beginning to have doubts about becoming an electrician, for which he had been studying at night. He didn't think he had enough attention to detail or concentration to do a good job. As it turned out, however, he would have no need for the Songfellows, Eddie Bond, or electrical work.

Memphis Recording Service

Elvis knew about Memphis Recording Service and had often passed it in his truck before he ever entered the little storefront at 706 Union Avenue. Its owner, Sam Phillips, was prominent in the Memphis music scene because he ran two small businesses.

Not a Phony

Elvis's first serious girlfriend, Dixie Locke, had this to say in Peter Guralnick's Last Train to Memphis:

"[Elvis] was not a phony, he was not a put-on, he was not a show-off, and once you were around him long enough to see him be himself, not just act the clown, anyone could see his real self, you could see his sweetness, you could see the humility, you could see the desire to please. . . .

He wasn't shy, he just had to be asked [to perform]— I think he just didn't want to impose. No one else ever did it, no one else had the nerve. He sang songs that were popular and a lot of the old blues type songs; he did some of the old spirituals, too. You know, it was funny. Right from the start it was as if he had a power over people, it was like they were transformed. It wasn't that he demanded anybody's attention, but they certainly reacted that way. . . . Like when Pastor Hamill walked up in the pulpit he commanded everyone's attention, it was the same thing with Elvis, it was always that way."

One was Memphis Recording Service, whose slogan was, "WE RECORD ANYTHING—ANYTIME—ANYWHERE." The firm rented audio equipment for taping weddings and other events. It also operated a small studio that made acetate discs, inexpensive versions of recordings. These acetates were often produced just for amateurs who wanted to hear their own voices. The cost was three dollars for a one-sided record, four dollars for two sides.

The other side of Phillips's operation was Sun Records, a pioneer company in the recording and distribution of black music. Sun was only one of dozens of small, independent labels around the country that struggled to make a profit from music outside the popular mainstream.

Sun recorded many artists who went on to fame, among them Bobby "Blue" Bland, Howlin' Wolf, B. B. King, and Big Walter Horton. Though it was a small operation, Sun was respected by musicians and businessmen who appreciated Phillips's honesty and commitment. A white man who loved and respected black music with an almost religious fervor, Phillips endured ridicule and hostility from many fellow Southerners because of his devotion to what they called "nigger music," but he kept at it. He once remarked, "It seemed to me that the Negroes were the only ones who had any freshness left in their music, and there was no place [besides Sun] in the South they could go to record."[14]

As a historian and champion of black music, Phillips was content to simply record and sell it to the best of his ability. But as a businessman who understood racial boundaries in the recording industry, Phillips knew that a white performer was his ticket to real success. He often remarked that he would make a fortune if he found a white singer who could sing with the passion, feeling, and intensity of a black artist.

He got his chance thanks to Marion Keisker, a former disc jockey who ran the office at Memphis Recording Service. It happened one afternoon in August or September of 1953, as she recalled, when Elvis walked in on his lunch break from Crown Electric.

"My Happiness"

Elvis wanted to make a record that day. According to one version of the story, it was supposed to be a birthday present for his mother. But Gladys's birthday was in April, so this is unlikely. Probably, he was simply inquisitive. As he put it later, "I went to Sun, paid my four bucks to the lady because I had a notion to find out what I really sounded like. I had been singing all my life and I was kind of curious."[15] Since he could have made a similar recording at a drugstore machine for only a quarter, he may have also been attracted by Phillips's reputation.

The studio was busy that day, so Elvis sat down in the outer office and politely waited his turn. As Keisker recalled, she struck up a conversation. "What do you sing?" she asked. "I sing all kinds," Elvis said. Thinking to label him as a ballad

crooner, hillbilly singer, or other type of performer, Keisker asked, "Who do you sound like?" And Elvis replied, "I don't sound like nobody."[16]

When it was Elvis's turn to record, he entered the small studio behind the front office. Phillips had built it himself and had personally modified and repaired the modest, well-worn equipment. As it happened, Phillips was not there that day, so Keisker ran the machines.

Accompanying himself on guitar, Elvis sang "My Happiness" and "That's When Your Heartaches Begin," two songs that had recently been made popular by a vocal group called the Ink Spots. When he heard it played back, Elvis wasn't satisfied with his voice, and he thought his guitar sounded bad. But Keisker felt differently; she heard something unusual in the young customer's voice.

She slipped a tape onto a spare reel-to-reel machine and made an extra copy of his recording. She told Elvis before he left that he had a good voice and that Phillips might be interested in using him on demo records. These demos, or demonstration records, were rough, quickly made, audio samples, used to present songs to potential clients—singers or record company executives, for example.

Phillips liked Elvis's voice but was not overwhelmed. When Elvis stopped at the studios again in January 1954, Phillips politely told him that there wasn't much demo work just then. Elvis was disappointed, but paid another four dollars and cut two more songs for himself: a ballad, "Casual Love Affair," and a country tune, "I'll Never Stand in Your Way." At the end of the session, Phillips took the kid's name and number and promised he'd be in touch.

A Failed Session

That June, Phillips received a demo record from a Nashville song promoter who wanted Phillips to consider it for release on Sun. The tune was a ballad called "Without You." Phillips loved both the song and the performance, and he wanted to release it exactly as it was. But no one knew where to find the singer, a drifter who happened to have been hanging around the Nashville studio. Phillips could still use the song, but he needed another singer.

Marion Keisker urged Phillips to call Elvis. Although the anonymous singer of "Without You" was black, the recording studio manager thought Elvis might be a good choice to sing the new version and found his phone number. Phillips got on the line and invited Elvis to give the song a try. Phillips later claimed that Elvis came running so quickly that he (Phillips) still had the phone in his hand when the aspiring singer came bursting through the door.

They set a date for the session, but the recording—with just Elvis and his guitar—didn't go smoothly. Elvis was nervous and couldn't get the song right. Phillips was patient and kind, urging him to relax and try different approaches, trying to pull emotion out of the young singer. But it was no use. Elvis finally lost his temper, frustrated that he couldn't achieve the same emotional power as the anonymous Nashville artist. He banged his fists against the studio walls and shouted, "I hate him!"[17]

Still, he refused to give up. It was an important moment for the nineteen-year-old singer, and one that was typical of his life in general. As writer Dave Marsh put it, "That his career didn't end on the spot can be attributed to that bizarre combination of luck, persistent arrogance, raw talent and gross ambition that sustained Elvis whenever he seemed about to sink."[18]

During a break, Phillips tried to cheer the kid up. So what if he couldn't sing "Without You"? What *could* he sing? Elvis repeated what he'd told Marion Keisker—that he could sing anything—and set out to prove it. He launched into an improvised session of virtually every song he knew—a little blues, a little gospel, a little pop. Sometimes he sang whole songs for Phillips, sometimes only brief bits.

The range and variety of this material impressed Phillips, and in Elvis's voice he heard a raw talent. Even though the "Without You" session was a failure, Phillips was enthused enough to introduce Elvis to a real working musician, a guitarist named Scotty Moore.

Scotty and Bill

Moore was twenty-one years old, newly married, and just out of the army when he met Elvis. Quiet but bright and ambitious, he worked in his brother's dry-cleaning plant during the week and played in a country band, the Starlite Wranglers, on the weekends.

Despite the difference in age, he and the older Sam Phillips were friends and musical soul mates. They shared a love of both blues and country, and they dreamed of finding a way to merge the two. Speaking of Phillips, Moore commented years later, "He knew there was a [musical] crossover coming. He foresaw it. I think that recording all those black artists had to give him an insight; he just didn't know where that insight would lead."[19]

An explosive Elvis Presley performs with his first band. Guitarist Scotty Moore and bassist Bill Black helped to create Elvis's unique style, which combined country, R&B, gospel, blues, and pop music.

When Phillips mentioned a promising singer named Elvis Presley, Scotty was intrigued—if only by Elvis's name, which he thought sounded like words from a science fiction book. One Sunday afternoon shortly after the "Without You" session, Elvis came over to Scotty's house. Moore recalled that Elvis had an elaborate DA and was wearing a pink suit and white shoes: "I thought my wife was going to go out the back door."[20] They sat around for two hours, playing a little of everything—from songs by country singer Marty Robbins to numbers made famous by big-band crooner Billy Eckstine. Bill Black, an outgoing neighbor of Moore's who played bass, wandered in and out, just listening.

Black and Moore thought Elvis had a good but not exceptional voice. They agreed he was too inexperienced for them, and Moore privately called him the "snotty-nosed kid . . . with the wild clothes."[21] Still, both Scotty and Bill agreed to come by for an audition Elvis had scheduled at Sun Records the next day.

Phillips liked what he had heard that afternoon. He encouraged the three to turn this casual rehearsal into weeks of hard, persistent work. They started getting together at Sun nearly every afternoon and evening after their day jobs ended.

It was an exciting experience. They weren't exactly sure what they wanted, but they knew that it would involve a combination of country, R&B, gospel, blues, and pop. There had been other such experiments: country singer Jimmie Rodgers had recorded with jazz trumpeter Louis Armstrong in the 1930s, and country and R&B singers occasionally made "cover versions" of each other's tunes. But there had never before been such a deep blending of styles. The Sun sessions were the first real attempt to cross so many musical boundaries at the same time.

The First Record

The encouragement and sharp ears of Sam Phillips were a blessing for the young musicians. Having access to the Sun studios had other advantages, as well. The concept of rehearsing in a recording studio, as opposed to live performance before an audience, was relatively new; tape recorders had been used commercially for less than a decade.

The machines were wonderfully liberating for musicians: they could record a song, listen back, analyze the results, and try it again immediately without worrying about audience reaction. The myth grew up in later years that Phillips and his young friends came up with their unique sound spontaneously. But it actually resulted from a great deal of patient hard work. As biographer Howard DeWitt noted, "Elvis' emergence [as a recording artist] was carefully rehearsed [and depended on] extensive planning by Sam Phillips."[22]

Several frustrating weeks passed, however, before the musicians found the right combination. The turning point came on July 5. While taking a break, Elvis began fooling with a blues tune, Arthur "Big Boy" Crudup's "That's All Right (Mama)." As Moore later recalled:

So Sweet and Young

Critic Dave Marsh reflects in this excerpt from Elvis *on the importance of Presley's first recording, "That's All Right (Mama)."*

"It is not the greatest record Presley ever made, and it is certainly not the bluesiest. But it has something else: a beautiful, flowing sense of freedom and release, Elvis' keening voice, so sweet and young, laying off the guitars, Scotty's hungry guitar choogling along neatly until it comes to the break, where it simply struts, definitive, mathematical, a precise statement of everything these young men are all about. Is it art? Is it history? Is it revolution? No one can know, not anymore, unless they were there to hear it before they'd heard any of the other music Elvis made or any of the rock & rollers who followed him. Is it pure magic, a distillation of innocence or just maybe a miracle, a band of cracker boys entering a state of cosmic grace? . . .

'That's All Right,' like the best of the later Sun material . . . sounds casual, the kind of music you could hear any day or every day, the kind of sound that has always been familiar but is still surprising. These men are reaching that elusive noise and once they have it in their grasp, they simply toy with it, flipping the thing back and forth among them as if they have been playing with it all their lives."

Elvis just started singing this song, jumping around and acting the fool, and then Bill picked up his bass, and he started acting the fool, too, and I started playing with them. Sam, I think, had the door to the control booth open—I don't know, he was either editing some tape, or doing something—and he stuck his head out and said, "What are you doing?" And we said, "We don't know." "Well, back up," he said, "try to find a place to start, and do it again."[23]

"Raw and Ragged"

Phillips was familiar with the tune but was amazed that Elvis had even *heard* of the relatively obscure Crudup. This, the blues, was the music Phillips loved most, and he heard in Elvis's voice a fresh, original take on it. He made the trio do the song again and again, urging them to simplify their sound. The chemistry, Phillips recalled later, was potent: he had the tangy guitar of Scotty Moore, the rhythmic pulse of bassist Bill Black, and Elvis in the middle, nervous but sounding fresh and unique.

At last Phillips was satisfied. The first time the group heard the final version played back, though, they were shocked. They liked it, but they couldn't figure out what it was besides weird. As Moore recalled:

It just sounded sort of raw and ragged. We thought it was exciting, but what

Elvis Presley holds a stack of acetate discs of "That's All Right (Mama)," his first recording. Elvis's fresh voice turned the old blues tune into a modern hit.

was it? It was just so completely different. But it just really flipped Sam—he felt it really had something. We just sort of shook our heads and said, "Well, that's fine, but good God, they'll run us out of town!"[24]

Phillips knew he had bagged a winner. The next day, he arranged to have his disc jockey friend Dewey Phillips (no relation) play an acetate of "That's All Right (Mama)" on his popular Memphis radio show—another event that helped put Elvis on a catapult to fame.

3 The Rise to Fame

If I stand still while I'm singin', I'm dead, man. I might as well go back to drivin' a truck.

Elvis Presley, 1956

Once you get used to it, if nobody comes up and asks for an autograph or if no one bothers you, then you start worrying. As long as they come round, you know that they still like you and it makes you feel good.

Elvis Presley, 1957

Dewey Phillips's *Red Hot and Blue* show on WHBQ was aimed at white listeners with a taste for the blues. Phillips loved the raw-sounding new song his friend Sam had produced, and only two days after its recording he debuted "That's All Right (Mama)."

Elvis was too nervous to listen. He tuned the family radio to Phillips's station, told his parents to listen, and went to the movies by himself. Meanwhile, at WHBQ the phone lines were lighting up with people demanding to know who the odd new singer was. Phillips played the song over and over that night.

Phillips also called the Presleys, hoping to interview Elvis. When Gladys told Phillips that her son was out, the DJ persuaded her to track him down. She and Vernon found Elvis at the theater and told him to hustle over to the station.

When a nervous Presley was interviewed on air later that evening, Phillips asked what high school he had graduated from. Phillips knew the answer would tell listeners, in those days of racial segregation in the schools, that Elvis was white. Nonetheless, many people who called in that night insisted that he had to be black.

Sam Phillips was encouraged by the positive response. But commercial records in the 1950s were released as singles. These vinyl discs, called 45s because they revolved at 45 revolutions per minute, had two sides—the "A" side had the hit, and the "B," or flip, side had a different tune. To release Elvis's record, Phillips needed a second song.

Within the next few days, Scotty, Bill, and Elvis had finished one. "Blue Moon of Kentucky," a hit for bluegrass star Bill Monroe in 1946, was originally a dignified waltz. In its new version, however, the song was transformed into a rocking mixture of blues and country, dominated by Elvis's shockingly lively voice. It has since been recorded by many artists in many ways.

The record was a hit when Phillips and a few other local DJs began playing it. By the song's official release date, July 19, it had racked up six thousand advance orders

Fans eager to receive autographs swarm around Elvis Presley. The release of his first record turned the young singer into an instant success.

—a very impressive figure for an unknown singer on a small label.

The First Live Shows

Presley's friends and acquaintances around town were amazed that he had actually cut a record—much less that it was a hit. Everyone knew about it and even strangers commented. His friend Kenneth Herman recalled, "We couldn't go anywhere with Elvis without someone hollering at us about his record."[25]

Elvis, who also couldn't quite believe it, was immensely proud of his achievement. He asked the owner of his favorite record store, the Blues Shop, to put his disc on the store's jukebox. He took a copy to the local skating rink and asked the manager to play it over the loudspeakers.

By the end of July, it was number three on the local sales charts. *Billboard* maga-zine, a journal for the music industry, gave it a positive review. But it remained strictly regional: disc jockeys outside Memphis thought it was either too country or too black—and too strange. As critic Dave Marsh remarked about Presley's early records in general, "Not very many DJs knew what to do with them. This sort of rock & roll was anything but trendy."[26]

Calling themselves the Blue Moon Boys, Elvis, Scotty, and Bill began appearing at little clubs around town. At these early shows, Scotty remarked later, Elvis was so nervous that you could hear his knees knocking. The band wasn't earning enough to make a living; Presley kept his job with Crown Electric, mostly because of pressure at home. Vernon often told Elvis that he thought guitar players were worthless.

The band's first big break was opening for country singer Slim Whitman at Memphis's Overton Park in mid-July. (The new singer was identified on posters as "Ellis

Presley.") The crowd loved Elvis's stage antics; Dewey Phillips recalled, "He went into 'That's All Right (Mama)' and started to shake and that damned auditorium just blew apart. He was nobody . . . but the people wouldn't let him leave."[27] But after two songs—both sides of their record—the band ran out of material and had to do "Blue Moon of Kentucky" again as an encore.

That concert effectively ended Scotty's association with his old band, the Starlite Wranglers. Other changes quickly came: Elvis felt confident enough to quit Crown Electric, join the musicians' union, and hire a manager. Scotty served briefly in this role, but didn't like it; then a local DJ took over, also briefly; he was soon replaced by Bob Neal.

The Opry and the Hayride

That fall, in October 1954, the band piled into Sam Phillips's Cadillac, strapped the string bass to the roof, and drove to Tennessee's other music capital, Nashville, for an appearance on the Grand Ole Opry. The Opry, which is still in existence, made weekly live broadcasts over station WSM. It was home base for country's

"I Just Fell into It, Really"

In an interview excerpted in Mick Farren's Elvis in His Own Words, *Elvis recalls his first major performance, the outdoor show at Overton Park, and its aftermath.*

"My very first appearance after I started recording, I was doing a show in Memphis where I started, a big show in an outdoor auditorium. I came to the stage and I was scared stiff. It was my first big appearance in front of an audience. I came out and I was doing a fast type tune, one of my first records, and everybody was hollering and I didn't know what they were hollering at. Then I came offstage and my manager told me that everyone was hollering because I was wiggling. So I did a little more and the more I did, the more I got.

I just fell into it, really. My daddy and I were laughing about it the other day. He looked at me and said, 'What happened, El? the last thing I can remember is I was working in a can factory, and you were driving a truck.' We all feel the same way about it still. . . .

I've been very lucky. . . . I happened to come along at a time in the music business when there was no trend. I was very lucky. The people were looking for something different and I was lucky. I came along just in time."

most important artists, including Patsy Cline, Loretta Lynn, Dolly Parton, and the team of George Jones and Tammy Wynette.

Elvis was nervous before the show. He told his bandmates that he would turn around and go home if they'd let him. As it turned out, his fears were justified—the band's appearance was a disaster. The Blue Moon Boys did not go over well with the live audience, a conservative crowd used to traditional country music. They didn't understand this strange new material at all. Jim Denny, the Opry's manager, hated the band; he swore that Presley would never again appear on his show, and advised him to go back to driving trucks. The band returned to Memphis in a blue mood.

Later that month, the band countered this failure with a successful appearance on the *Louisiana Hayride* program. The *Hayride*, which came on every Saturday night from KWKH in Shreveport, Louisiana, was a jumping-off point for many famous musicians, including the most influential country singer of all, Hank Williams. Its audience was generally younger and less stuffy than the Opry crowd—and they loved the Blue Moon Boys.

The *Hayride* specialized in finding promising young talent, and after just one appearance Elvis was asked to become a regular member of the show. The one-year contract called for the band to play every Saturday night. Elvis got eighteen dollars per appearance; Scotty and Bill each got twelve dollars. It seemed like a fortune.

Besides gaining steady work as a performer, Presley made important connections through the *Hayride*. D. J. Fontana was the staff drummer for the radio show. He backed up Elvis's appearances there and later became the band's regular drummer.

Elvis and the Blue Moon Boys appear on the Louisiana Hayride. *After the band's initial success, Elvis was given a one-year contract to become a permanent member of the show.*

"You Can't Help but Move to It"

In a 1950s interview, reprinted in Mick Farren's Elvis in His Own Words, *Elvis reflects on his music and its effect on people.*

"Rock and roll has been around for many years. It used to be called rhythm and blues. And as far back as I can remember it's been very big, although in the last five years it's gotten much bigger. But personally I don't think it'll ever die completely out because they're gonna have to get something mighty good to take its place.

Rock and roll music, if you like it and if you feel it, you can't help but move to it. That's what happens to me, I can't help it.

I don't see that any type of music would have any bad influence on people. It's only music. I can't figure it out . . . I mean, how would rock and roll music make anybody rebel against their parents?

I've been blamed for just about everything wrong in this country. . . . I'm vulgar, they say. I wouldn't do anything vulgar in front of anybody, 'specially children. My folks didn't bring me up that way.

I don't do anything bad when I work. I just move to the music 'count of it's the way I feel it. I hear it and I gotta move."

Another important connection was Oscar Davis. Davis was a public-relations veteran doing advance work for a flamboyant concert promoter named Colonel Tom Parker. Through Davis, Colonel Parker caught wind of the hot new commodity named Elvis Presley, and the seeds of a legendary partnership were sown.

"Good Rockin' Tonight"

By the time Elvis joined the *Hayride,* a second single, "Good Rockin' Tonight," was working its way to number three on the Memphis charts. Despite another favorable write-up in *Billboard,* however, it did poorly outside Memphis.

"Good Rockin' Tonight" was an intense R&B tune originally recorded by Wynonie Harris in 1948. The flip side continued the strategy of contrasting earthy R&B with a more mellow country-pop sound. In this case, "I Don't Care if the Sun Don't Shine" had originally been a hit for pop singer Dean Martin. Martin was one of Elvis's heroes, and the influence of Martin's lazy crooning on Elvis is clear in this recording.

"His Hair Is His Crowning Glory"

In Elvis World, *Jane and Michael Stern describe Elvis's appearance in performance.*

"His face is as startling as his body. In repose [rest], the profile is Michelangelo's David: classical Grecian nose flattened and straight as a rule, venting hot breath above pouty lips. But it is seldom in repose. The mouth twitches and grimaces, flickering from a sneer to a boyish smile. The eyelids, low and lush, tinted by nature a pale iridescent brown, and by mascara a sooty black, hang heavy over pale blue eyes that shimmy in and out of focus.

Like buttercream frosting on a cake, his hair is his crowning glory. Depending on the month and the performance, it ranges from light brown to black. What is constant is the great gob of pomade [hair oil], a glistening brilliantine of good-ol'-boy viscosity [stickiness] like Dixie Peach or Lover's Moon, raked into the locks so thick that you can count the furrows dug by the tines of the comb.

The tonsorial pyrotechnics [hair fireworks] are not just a hairdo, no mere wad of mane to keep the head warm and the hat cushioned. Hair is his trademark and his strength. It has a life of its own, more than the sum of the parts that critics inventory and fans dote over—the sideburns, the wave, the fenders, the duck's ass.

Like the man to whose scalp it is attached, the hair breaks loose onstage. Appearing first as a unitary [single] loaf of high-rise melted vinyl etched with grooves along the side, it detonates at the strike of the first chord. It hangs low and dirty, it whips to the beat, it clings like a greedy lover to the sweaty skin on Elvis's neck."

Both sides of the record are masterpieces of simplicity. Sam Phillips recalled later that he focused on paring the sound to a minimum: "Everything had to be a stinger. To me every one of those sessions was like I was filming *Gone with the Wind.*"

Scotty Moore added, "It was almost a total rhythm thing. With only the three of us we had to make every note count." Moore also commented that the work was hard but enjoyable: "Sam's one organizing principle was that it had to be fun." [28]

Through the winter, Presley and his band made scattered appearances throughout the South and Southwest. Admission generally was one dollar, with half off for kids. Audience response was strong from the beginning—sometimes positive, with the whole audience cheering like crazy, and sometimes hostile. More than once, the band had to duck out of a hall quickly to avoid angry young men who thought Elvis was exciting their girlfriends a little too much.

Undaunted, Elvis continued to perfect his onstage persona, a sexy combination of danger and innocence, and the band honed their show into a tight, fast performance. Presley used trial and error to discover what worked. If he happened to make an accidental movement onstage that created screams, he did it again the next night. If something special he had planned got no reaction, he simply dropped it.

By this time, a little money was beginning to come in. Neal set up new offices on Union Street for Presley, organized a fan club, and ordered special stationery in Elvis's favorite colors, pink and black. Meanwhile, Elvis bought a '51 Lincoln, painted "Elvis Presley—Sun Records" on the sides, and drove it to gigs until Bill wrecked it. More cars came and went, including a pink Ford and a pink Cadillac.

Besides the weekly *Hayride* shows, the band played all over the South and came home to rest and rehearse. Presley often appeared as part of a package tour—that is, a show featuring several famous performers along with up-and-coming artists. More and more, Elvis—billed as "the Hillbilly Cat" or "the King of Western Bop"—was stealing the show from the established musicians.

The First Big Tour

The band's next single was "Milkcow Blues Boogie," originally popularized by country-swing star Bob Wills. The flip side, "You're a Heartbreaker," was the first original song Elvis recorded. This record proved that Elvis's appeal was not yet a sure thing; it sold poorly and was not even reviewed in *Billboard*.

Nonetheless, Elvis's fourth release continued the pattern of combining a rhythm and blues rocker ("Baby, Let's Play House") and a country tune ("I'm Left, You're Right, She's Gone"). This one was Presley's commercial breakthrough, selling widely and whipping up a storm of enthusiasm all over the South. Dave Marsh wrote of Elvis's confident performance on it: "[I]t's hard to believe that only a year before Elvis had been pounding the wall at Sun, cursing the anonymous singer whose quality he could not match."[29]

The group had saved for months to take a trip to New York in order to audition for Arthur Godfrey's popular television show. When they finally made the journey north, the woman who held the audition rudely rejected the band. They never even got to meet the show's star, much less appear on the program.

So they kept on the road. At least the money was getting better. The band was now making $200–$400 a night; after expenses and Bob Neal's 15 percent were taken out, half went to Elvis and a quarter each to Scotty and Bill. Presley could now afford to move himself and his parents into their first real house, a modest place on Lamar Avenue in Memphis. They were still renting, but it was a real home they didn't have to share.

In May, Presley appeared in a new package tour, with Hank Snow, Slim Whitman, Faron Young, and the Carter Sisters starring. By now, people were beginning to recognize Elvis's name; this three-week jaunt through the South was his first tour as something more than a Memphis-area phenomenon.

The first real Elvis riot—a scenario that would become commonplace—occurred in Jacksonville, Florida, just after the Fourth of July. At one point, Elvis grinned and said to the girls in the crowd of fourteen thousand that he would meet them all backstage. The result was pandemonium—Presley's jacket, shirt, and shoes were ripped off by screaming fans before the whole band could be hustled away.

On the Edge of the Big Time

One person who clearly noticed the building excitement was Colonel Parker, who had been contacted by Neal to help book some of Presley's performances. Parker was already managing stars like Eddy Arnold and Hank Snow, and he had better contacts and more experience than Neal.

The Leaf Gimmick

In Mick Farren's Elvis in His Own Words, *Elvis comments on the ingenuity of his manager, Colonel Tom Parker.*

"One morning I looked out of my bedroom window on the second floor facing the highway, and spotted a man picking up leaves outside the stone fence, and stuffing them in a valise.

I told my manager, Colonel Tom Parker, and he went out to check on things. He asked the man what he was doing with the leaves and the man said he'd got a big thing going up in Buffalo, New York, selling the leaves for souvenirs. He was selling them for 10 dollars apiece.

The Colonel admired the man's ingenuity so much, he let him go. The fella kept right on picking up leaves—just the choice ones—and putting them in his bag.

The Colonel got to thinking about the 'leaf gimmick' as he called it, and contacted the local Memphis radio station. He invited them over to come out and rake up 10 or 12,000 leaves and offer them as prizes in various Elvis Presley contests. My discs got a bigger than ever radio play and those leaves went like wildfire."

As Elvis's popularity soared, he was increasingly mobbed by fans and practically every record label in the country vied for the chance to buy his contract from Sun Records.

For a long time the Colonel had been unsure about taking a more active role in Presley's career, but the Jacksonville riot opened his eyes. After that, Parker attached himself firmly to the rising star. As biographer Peter Guralnick put it, "By the time the show got to Richmond three days later, it was as if Elvis had never been anything but the Colonel's boy."[30]

Elvis was dazzled by the Colonel's promises of stardom. The singer held off on signing any contracts, however, because his parents weren't sure they trusted Parker. Gladys didn't like the Colonel, and the Jacksonville riot had upset her. She was still hoping that Elvis would settle down, marry, and start a good, solid business; she liked the idea of a furniture shop.

Wisely, the Colonel did not press the issue. Instead, he announced that they would hold off until Gladys could be assured.

When Elvis returned to Memphis, the band recorded a new single. One side was a minor country song, "I Forgot to Remember to Forget." But the other was "Mystery Train," a masterful blend of two classic songs: the Carter Family's hillbilly tune "Worried Man Blues" and the deep blues of Little Junior Parker's "Mystery Train." Critic Dave Marsh called Elvis's version a bold slap in the face to the bland pop music of the 1950s: "the most exciting music he recorded at Sun, and maybe ever . . . a massive gesture of defiance and arrogance."[31]

"Mystery Train" was the last single Elvis ever recorded for Sun. Already, there were rumors that Elvis and "his people" (meaning the Colonel) thought that Sam Phillips's little label was not adequate to handle the big star that Elvis was sure to become. Virtually every record label in the country was nibbling to see if his contract could be bought.

It was an exciting time for Presley. He was making good money, getting lots of attention, and moving fast. He was appearing with some of country's biggest entertainers and had attracted the attention of a powerful manager. In little more than a year, he had come further than he had ever dared hope.

He was ready for the big time.

4 The Big Time

The Colonel seldom missed a bet.
> writer Jerry Hopkins

We're the perfect combination. The Colonel's an old carny, and me, I'm off the wall.
> Elvis Presley, 1956

It wasn't his records that ultimately made Elvis Presley a household dream and nightmare; it was those wild-eyed TV performances of his records, sheer, paralyzing intensity brought straight into comfortable homes.

> writer Dave Marsh

Tom Parker knew that Elvis would sign a management contract only if his parents approved, so he set out to win their trust. He convinced Vernon that Sun Records wasn't competent to handle Elvis, and he told Gladys that Sun was working her boy too hard. He also sweetened the deal with ready supplies of cash. A friend of the Presley family, Jim Denson, recalled, "The Colonel always gave Vernon one-hundred-dollar bills when there was a problem. The hundred-dollar bills were flowing like water."[32]

The strategy worked. In August 1955, the Presleys and Parker signed the "special adviser" contract. Parker immediately began serious negotiations with record companies on behalf of Elvis.

RCA, the biggest company, was his first choice. Parker had managed two RCA stars, Hank Snow and Eddy Arnold, and he knew many executives within the company. Also, RCA had good TV and movie connections, a direction Parker and Presley wanted to pursue.

In November, Parker announced that RCA was buying Elvis's contract for $40,000; there would be $35,000 for Sam Phillips and $5,000 for Elvis. This was the highest fee ever paid for a popular entertainer, and the news stunned the industry. Elvis was now on the biggest label in the land, with enough money invested in him (about one hundred times more than normal for an unknown act) to ensure that RCA would heavily promote him.

The Colonel

After Vernon and Gladys Presley and Sam Phillips, Tom Parker was the most influential person in Elvis's career. He had more to do with making Elvis a household word than anyone besides Presley himself.

The Colonel and Elvis would have been successes even if they had never met; to-

Tom Parker and his protégé, Elvis Presley. Under Parker's able management, Elvis contracted with RCA—the biggest music label in the country.

gether, they were unstoppable. Parker liked to say that when he first saw "the boy," the only thing Elvis had was a million dollars' worth of talent—but that after they joined forces Elvis had a million dollars, too.

Parker loved to tell stories about his rough West Virginia childhood, when (so he said) he hustled for dollars in his uncle's carnival. Some of his carnival stories were true, but Parker did not grow up in West Virginia.

He was born Andreas van Kuijik in the Netherlands. Intrigued by wild stories about America told by a seafaring uncle, eighteen-year-old Andreas sailed there in 1927. He fell in love with the lively variety of the American South; combining this with his lifelong love of circuses and carnivals, Andreas decided he would return one day to seek his fortune in American show business.

Back in America for a second visit in 1929, he hitchhiked around the South and eventually enlisted in the U. S. Army under the name Andre van Kuijik. The fact that the heavily accented youth was able to talk his way into the military despite his lack of a birth certificate was a measure of Parker's growing ability to bluster his way through any situation.

After his discharge the young man worked in carnivals, selling refreshments, operating merry-go-rounds and hustling sideshow customers across America. He held a variety of other jobs as well, including dogcatcher and operator of a pet cemetery. He called himself Tom Parker, after a captain he had known in the service.

By the time he entered Presley's life, Parker had become a flamboyant music promoter with a slight accent, a fondness for cigars, and a genius for public relations. In 1948, the governor of Louisiana, Jimmie Davis, bestowed the title of honorary colonel on him. Davis had once been a country singer-songwriter who knew Parker well. After that, everyone called Parker "the Colonel."

Spending a Hundred Dollars to Beat You Out of a Dollar

In this excerpt from Last Train to Memphis, *Peter Guralnick discusses Colonel Parker's unusual drives.*

"He kept nearly everyone, even his closest associates, at arm's length. 'You have one fault,' he told his brother-in-law, Bitsy Mott. 'You make too many friends.' His cold eyes belied his occasional warmheartedness; his absolute honesty in business affairs conflicted with the opportunism that always drove him to come out on top not just in formal dealings but in day-to-day affairs as well (he would spend a hundred dollars, it was said, to beat you out of a dollar). 'He got a helluva kick,' Chet Atkins declared, 'out of getting someone to pick up the check. Or out of just beating you in a deal—any kind of a deal.' He was capable of real generosity, but more than anything else he loved the game. As [business associate] Gabe Tucker observed . . . he never really left the carnival world, in which 'they speak a different language. All of them is just like the Colonel; they'll cut your throat just to watch you bleed. But they've got their own laws, it's a game with them, to outsmart you, you're always the pigeon to them.' In Gabe's view . . . everyone else in the Colonel's estimation was a little bit of a fool."

Although his later fame probably would have let him straighten out his illegal status, Parker never bothered to become a naturalized U. S. citizen. His lack of a passport was probably a major reason why his most famous client, Elvis Presley, never toured overseas. This no doubt hampered Presley's career; as writer Howard DeWitt put it, "From day one with the Colonel . . . Elvis was basically confined in a career straight jacket."[33] Despite this obstacle, the Colonel managed to pull in plenty of money over the years for himself and "the boy."

The carnival mentality—anything for a buck, and there's a sucker born every minute—stayed with Parker all his life. Once, when his client Eddy Arnold was too sick to sing, Parker told the show's producer that he had a terrific animal act he could substitute. He then set an electric hot plate under a chicken cage and created a dancing chicken act. Parker claimed that he got away with this stunt for two days before Arnold recovered.

All his life, Parker was a tough negotiator and a relentless tracker of money. Especially after Presley moved to the world of big money, the Colonel directed his client's career with an iron fist and a keen eye for the buck. Producer Hal Wallis, a veteran of many Elvis movies, once re-marked of Parker: "I'd rather try and close a deal with the devil."[34]

Parker's diligence helped Elvis, of course, but throughout their years together Parker also used his insider's knowledge of the music business to take advantage of his trusting client. Their "special adviser" agreement allowed Parker to make deals without consulting Elvis. It allowed Parker to reject movies and songs that Elvis liked in favor of inferior but better-paying material. Since Parker loved to keep his plans secret, Elvis never knew from day to day exactly where his career was headed.

And then there was the question of how the money was split. No one knows exactly how much the Colonel received;

Tom Parker became Elvis's "special adviser" in August 1955. The Colonel, as he was called, was a flamboyant music promoter and a tough negotiator who guided Elvis to stardom.

he always told reporters it was 25 percent, but after Presley's death a lawsuit brought by the singer's estate revealed that the amount was closer to half. Elvis's daughter Lisa Marie had to sue Parker to recover millions of dollars that had been illegally withdrawn from Presley's earnings.

"Heartbreak Hotel"

On January 10, 1956, two days after his twenty-first birthday, Elvis entered an RCA recording studio for the first time. With him in Nashville was his regular band, plus pianist Floyd Cramer and members of the Jordanaires vocal group. Guitar legend Chet Atkins coproduced the session with Steve Sholes, the RCA vice president who had signed Presley.

Everyone was tense, even the usually genial Bill Black. The Blue Moon Boys were used to the cozy setup at Sun and had never been in a big studio before. The session was just as nerve-wracking for producer Sholes. Many within the music industry thought that RCA had backed a loser; Elvis had a couple of hot singles, but his success was not at all a sure thing. It was up to Sholes to produce a hit.

Presley impressed Sholes with his near-photographic memory for lyrics; after just the second take of an unknown song, Elvis knew the words cold. Sholes later recalled, "Sometimes . . . I'd say, 'Gee, Elvis, I think you made a mistake in the lyrics there.' And he'd say, 'I don't think I did, Mr. Sholes.' And I'd look at the damn sheet and I'd find he was right."[35]

Gradually the tension faded and the band cut five usable songs over two days. Three were new tunes, never before recorded: "Heartbreak Hotel," "I Was the One," and "I'm Counting on You." The other two were cover versions of tunes that were already popular: Ray Charles's "I've Got a Woman" and the Drifters's "Money Honey." The overall sound was similar to the Sun singles, though the addition of the backup singers and pianist gave it a softer edge.

"Heartbreak Hotel" was a dark and gloomy song, and Sholes was hesitant about releasing it as Elvis's first big-label single. But he did, and its haunting lyrics and eerie reverb caught the public's ear. It was in the national Top Forty within a month. The gamble paid off.

A soulful Elvis taps his guitar during a July 1956 recording session in the RCA studios.

The First TV Appearances

The immediate impact of "Heartbreak Hotel," Presley's first national radio hit, led to interest from television. At the end of January, Elvis made his first TV appearances, on a Saturday night show starring swing-band leaders Tommy and Jimmy Dorsey. The money wasn't great but, as the Colonel pointed out, more people would be exposed to Elvis on TV than would hear him on the *Louisiana Hayride* if he sang there for the rest of his life.

Television was by now the dominant form of American entertainment. In 1950 there had been only 1.5 million sets in the country; many people still preferred the movies or live entertainment. But by 1956 TV was king; there were over 50 million sets in the country, and Parker knew that each one had a cluster of viewers eager to see what all the Hillbilly Cat fuss was about.

There were few in the audience at the New York theater where the first Dorsey broadcast originated; a storm had hit the city and not many people were on the streets. Those who did attend, and those who watched the January 28 show, saw performances by jazz singer Sarah Vaughan, comic and banjoist Gene Sheldon, and a startling Elvis Presley.

After the smooth sound of the Dorsey orchestra, Presley's loud, aggressive little band was a shock. Elvis, as writer Peter Guralnick put it, came onstage looking "as if he'd been shot out of a cannon." His voice was raw and powerful, and his whole body shook as if wracked by convulsions. It was a fierce, uncontrolled moment of energy and joy; as Guralnick put it, "What you take away from [the performance] is the

A true entertainer, Elvis would captivate audiences with his powerful voice and his often shocking movements.

His final appearance on the Dorsey show, in March, featured "Heartbreak Hotel" and a new tune by Elvis's friend Carl Perkins, "Blue Suede Shoes." In just a few weeks Presley's television presence had become even more self-assured. At the end of this performance, he looked out, amused, at the screaming audience and then grinned with delight. The slightest move he made—a twitch, a raised eyebrow—would cause a flood of screams. He was a star, and he knew it.

That night, the band left New York by car for California. Elvis stayed a few extra days in New York for interviews, then flew to meet the band. Parker had arranged for "the boy" to make more television appearances and take a Hollywood screen test.

Hollywood and Vegas

By the time Elvis hit Hollywood, the entertainment industry was no longer regarding him as a hillbilly freak. "Heartbreak Hotel" had sold nearly a million copies, and it was closing in on the number-one positions of all three main sales charts—pop, country, and R&B. His first long-playing album, meanwhile, was about to become RCA's first million-dollar LP.

In California, Elvis appeared on comedian Milton Berle's popular TV show. He took part in a silly comedy sketch with Berle, who pretended to be Elvis's twin brother Melvin. If this cut close to the bone for a man whose real-life twin had died at birth, Elvis seemed not to show it; he remained good-natured and polite. Presley also made a screen test for producer Hal Wallis. Wallis was favorably

sheer enjoyment of the moment. *Elvis Presley is on top of the world.*"[36]

On the second Dorsey show, Elvis made the unusual move of singing songs that were not current singles. Instead, he sang Little Richard's "Tutti Frutti" and an as-yet unknown number, "Baby, Let's Play House." Back on the road, the momentum from these first TV appearances was mounting. It also took its toll on Elvis's health: in February, he collapsed while loading band instruments in Jacksonville, Florida. He was treated for exhaustion at a local hospital, but checked out before morning—because, he joked to reporters, the nurses wouldn't let him get any rest.

Giving Up Rebellion

Dave Marsh reflects on Presley's willingness to give up rebellion and embrace the world of mainstream pop music in this excerpt from Elvis.

"Consider Elvis in January 1956. He was twenty-one years old, the product of the poorest part of the poorest and most insular part of the nation. He was a spoiled only child who had never been asked to make difficult choices. . . .

This Elvis had no role models. Other pop singers were not rebelling against the system and the few rebels he did know were country-music honky-tonkers in the Hank Williams mold, clearly destined for self-destruction. . . .

Further weighing against the possibility of rebellion was Elvis' idea of what was 'practical.' This reflected an instinctive knowledge that it was better not to challenge one's superiors directly, that the liberties that had been granted could easily be taken away. Elvis regarded pop music as a job—'I became a singer because I didn't want to sweat'—and he certainly did not want to lose it.

Then, too, there was Elvis' uncommon mixture of arrogance and humility—if he were bold enough to imagine that he could convert any trashy song into something palatable, he was also humble enough to suspect that he might just deserve nothing better than these tepid little tunes. There can be no doubt, of course, that Elvis understood perfectly well the mediocrity of the songs he was asked to sing. But Elvis did look at music as a job; his primary goal was always money. In that respect, even the worst material was wildly successful; people bought the hell out of it.

They bought it because he was extraordinarily good and because what he did was so liberating. It was precisely 'Heartbreak Hotel' and the other hits Elvis recorded in 1956 . . . that were responsible for inciting what we now recognize as the rock & roll audience into self-awareness for the first time. It is foolish to contend that Elvis was artistically less powerful once he left Sam Phillips' tutelage, because he demonstrated so pragmatically that he was so much *more* powerful."

impressed, and plans were made for a three-movie contract.

While Elvis's California trip was a success, his next big engagement was not. A two-week gig in April at the New Frontier hotel in Las Vegas stands as one of the rare occasions of miscalculation by the Colonel. Vegas was simply not ready for Elvis. "The Atomic Powered Singer," as he was billed, was too wild for the conservative audiences. They walked out in droves; after the first week, the Colonel admitted defeat and tore up Elvis's contract for the New Frontier gig.

But the engagement did have some positive aspects. For one thing, the New Frontier crowd was quiet, and it was the first time in months the band had been able to hear themselves when they played out of tune.

More importantly, Elvis heard a lounge act, Freddie Bell and the Bellboys, perform a song first recorded by blues singer Big Mama Thornton in 1953. Elvis loved the tune's witty lyrics and melody, by the up-and-coming team of Jerry Leiber and Mike Stoller, and he immediately incorporated it into his repertoire. "Hound Dog" would become one of Elvis's most famous and controversial songs.

Elvis returned home for a brief vacation—six days, his longest period of rest in months. He spent it hanging out with friends, including a new girlfriend: June Juanico, a beauty queen from Biloxi, Mississippi.

Then it was off to California for another appearance on the Berle show. The raunchy version of "Hound Dog" that he performed there brought howls of protest from outraged parents, clergymen, and commentators all across the country. But Elvis and the Colonel were laughing all

the way to the bank—there were Presley records now on top of all three national sales charts.

"Hound Dog"

In late June, Elvis went to New York to appear on still another top TV program, the *Steve Allen Show.* Allen, a comedian, jazz composer, and pianist, had long been critical of rock and roll. He wanted to make Presley more acceptable to the general

A tuxedo-clad Elvis Presley appeared on the Steve Allen Show *in late June 1956. Here, Allen applauds the young singer's new look.*

public by dressing him in a tuxedo and blue suede shoes. He was not allowed to dance, but was told to stand still. Furthermore, instead of appearing with his band, Elvis had to sing "Hound Dog" to a real basset hound.

Marketing, Marketing, Marketing

Colonel Parker initiated the biggest marketing campaign of an entertainment figure in history, as Jerry Hopkins points out in this excerpt from Elvis.

"So pervasive was the marketing [that] if one of Elvis's fans bought one of everything, she could, upon arising in the morning, pull on some Elvis Presley bobbysocks, Elvis Presley shoes, an Elvis Presley skirt and Elvis Presley blouse, an Elvis Presley sweater, hang an Elvis Presley charm bracelet from one wrist, put an Elvis Presley handkerchief in her Elvis Presley purse and head for school, where she might swap some Elvis Presley bubble gum cards before class, where she would take notes with an Elvis Presley pencil.

After school she might change into Elvis Presley Bermuda shorts, Elvis Presley blue jeans (which were not blue but black, trimmed in white and carried Elvis's face on a pocket tag) or Elvis Presley toreador pants, and either write an Elvis Presley pen pal (whose address she got from an Elvis Presley magazine) or play an Elvis Presley game, while drinking an Elvis Presley soft drink. And before going to bed in her Elvis Presley knit pajamas, she might write in her Elvis Presley diary, using an Elvis Presley ball-point pen, listen to 'Hound Dog' a final ten times, then switch out the light to watch the Elvis Presley picture that glowed in the dark.

That wasn't all. There were Elvis Presley photographs (glossy eight-by-tens and wallet size), belts, bolo ties, gloves, mittens, novelty hats, T-shirts, neckerchiefs, necklaces, statues and plaster-of-paris busts, bookends, guitars, lipstick (in Hound Dog Orange, Heartbreak Hotel Pink and Tutti Frutti Red), colognes, stuffed hound dogs, dancing dolls, greeting cards, pins, sneakers, buttons, photograph albums, phonographs, Ivy League pants, Ivy League girls' shirts, pillows, combs, hairbrushes and twenty-nine other things."

Elvis went along with these demeaning attempts to take the sting out of his act. His mother had taught him to accept whatever situation he was given and to cooperate with authority. Privately, however, he was angry and humiliated.

Allen's attempt to "sweeten" Elvis backfired. For days after Presley's tuxedoed appearance, fans picketed the studios with signs reading, "We Want the *Real* Elvis!" The resulting publicity made Elvis bigger than ever. And the nation's top TV host, Ed Sullivan, who had rejected Presley earlier in the year, changed his mind and offered him $50,000 for three shows—three times what Sullivan had ever paid anyone.

While in New York for the Allen show, Elvis recorded his version of "Hound Dog." The singer's need for perfection in the studio was especially apparent at this session.

The band did take after take, but Elvis didn't like what he heard and kept asking to do it again. Alfred Wertheimer, a photographer documenting the session, recalled, "In his own reserved manner, he kept control, he made himself responsible. When somebody else made a mistake, he sang off-key. The offender picked up the cue. He never criticized anyone, never got mad at anybody but himself. He'd just say, 'Okay, fellas, I goofed.'"[37] After twenty-six takes, producer Steve Sholes wanted to quit, but Elvis wasn't satisfied until the thirty-third take.

This session was followed by three weeks of vacation at home and in Biloxi, where Presley went to visit June. By this time, his growing fame meant he was never alone. Every time Presley walked out of his Biloxi hotel, his car was covered with love notes and the windows smeared with messages written in lipstick. Hundreds of people were waiting for autographs. He refused to say no to anyone, saying always that he would be nowhere without his fans.

Back in Memphis there was further evidence of a growing devotion. Presley would stand for hours every day signing autographs in the driveway of 1034 Audubon Drive, the modest ranch house he had bought for himself and his parents. When he was out of town, fans would ask Gladys if they could wipe their hankies across the dust on his car. The Presleys never needed to mow their lawn; it was picked clean by fans seeking souvenir grass blades to take home.

Sometimes the attention was unwanted. When a crowd formed around Elvis at a Memphis gas station, the attendant asked him to move. Presley was slow to leave, and the attendant slapped him. Elvis decked the guy, and after another attendant pulled a knife the police were called. The courts found the first attendant guilty, but Elvis was unhappy. He told reporters that he would regret the incident all his life, and he complained that he could barely even leave his house anymore.

More Triumphs

In many ways, Presley was still a country boy. He remarked to the Memphis *Press-Scimitar* that he didn't want people to think his ego was inflating because of all the attention. "More than anything else," he said, "I want the folks back home to think right of me. Just because I managed to do a little something, I don't want anyone . . . to think I got the big head."[38]

But the fans were going crazy. At an outdoor show on the Fourth of July (officially declared "Elvis Presley Day" by the mayor of Memphis), the ecstatic crowd roared so loudly that according to some reports, extra sleeping pills were passed out to patients in nearby hospitals. When Presley finally appeared he assured fans that "those people in New York" were not going to change him at all. He proceeded to give them a triumphant performance that proved, in full view of his family and his hometown, that he was succeeding on a grand scale.

That fall and winter, Presley re-created that shining moment nationwide, when he made three appearances on the premiere TV program in the land: the *Ed Sullivan*

"No Discernible Singing Ability"

Mainstream critics were appalled at the rawness of Presley's early TV appearances. Typical was Jack Gould, writing in the New York Times *following the singer's second appearance on Milton Berle's show (as quoted in Jerry Hopkins's* Elvis).

"Mr. Presley made another television appearance last night on the Milton Berle show over Channel 4. Indeed, the entire program revolved around the boy. Attired in the familiar oversize jacket and open shirt which are almost the uniform of the contemporary youth who fancies himself as terribly sharp, he might possibly be classified as an entertainer. Or, perhaps quite as easily, as an assignment for a sociologist.

Mr. Presley has no discernible singing ability. His specialty is rhythm songs which he renders in an undistinguished whine; his phrasing, if it can be called that, consists of the stereotyped variations that go with a beginner's aria in a bathtub. For the ear he is an unutterable bore, not nearly so talented as Frankie Sinatra back in the latter's rather hysterical days at the Paramount Theater. . . .

From watching Mr. Presley it is wholly evident that his skill lies in another direction. He is a rock-and-roll variation of one of the most standard acts in show business: the virtuoso of the hootchy-kootchy. His one specialty is an accented movement of the body that heretofore has been primarily identified with the repertoire of the blonde bombshells of the burlesque runway. The gyration never had anything to do with the world of popular music and still doesn't."

An ecstatic Elvis Presley rehearses for his second appearance on the Ed Sullivan Show. *Elvis received $50,000 for his three appearances on the popular TV program.*

Show. These famous performances, more than any other single event, cemented Elvis's lasting fame. Elvis was inspiring dozens of rivals, but he was without question the champ.

The first show in September was watched by over 80 percent of the viewing public: fifty-four million people, more than any program in history. A second appearance in October brought torrents of protest about Elvis's supposedly lewd dancing. The protest led to Sullivan's decision that for the third appearance, on January 6, 1957, the singer would be on camera from only the waist up.

"Elvis the Pelvis," as he'd been dubbed by the press, used the restriction to his advantage. Dressed in a gold lamé jacket, he stood relatively still and wiggled just his shoulders and eyebrows as he sang. He knew this would bring as many screams as his usual dance steps. He grinned as each tiny movement devastated the fans; he was clearly playing with the crowd, teasing it mercilessly and having fun.

Sullivan, who had publicly scorned Presley earlier, called the singer back onstage afterward to hug him and say, "I wanted to say to Elvis Presley and the country that this is a real decent, fine boy."[39] Sullivan may or may not have meant it, but Elvis and the Colonel were again laughing all the way to the bank. Parker set an absurdly high price for further TV appearances by his client, and Presley would not appear there again until 1960.

But no matter; by now, television was not the big time. Elvis was about to launch an even more successful career—in the movies.

5 The Early Movies

When he started, he couldn't spell 'Tennessee.' Now he owns it.
                    comedian Bob Hope

Well, sir, I've been very lucky. I happened to come along at a time in the music business when there was no trend. The people were looking for something different, and I was lucky. I came along just in time.
                    Elvis Presley, 1958

Colonel Parker had set up a deal with Hal Wallis for three pictures starring "the boy." Elvis would get $100,000 for the first, $150,000 for the second, and $200,000 for the third. These were shockingly high figures for an untried screen talent, but it was justified: the profit on Elvis movies over the years averaged about ten times the cost.

Elvis spent much of the summer and fall of 1956 making his first movie: a Western, *The Reno Brothers*, renamed *Love Me Tender* in honor of the song he introduced in it. A drama set just after the Civil War, it has—unlike future Elvis movies—only a little music.

Presley's near-photographic memory served him well on the set. By the first day of shooting, he not only knew all his lines but everyone else's, too. And he had a sharp instinct about the job, though he had never formally acted. "I've made a study of Marlon Brando," he told a reporter. "I've made a study of poor Jimmy [James] Dean. I've made a study of myself, and I know why girls, at least the young 'uns, go for us. We're sullen, we're broodin', we're something of a menace. I don't understand it exactly, but that's what the girls like in men."[40]

Generally, the cast and crew were impressed with Elvis's polite, professional attitude; this was not the wild Hillbilly Cat they'd been expecting. He told the people around him that he was humbled by his situation. He felt that God had given him a special gift, and that he had to be nice to people or God would take it back.

The film was finished in time for a Thanksgiving release. From the beginning, the Colonel wisely set the release dates of Elvis movies to coincide with school holidays. He knew that Elvis fans were mostly schoolgirls, and that given free time they'd see his movies again and again.

Three thousand kids were lined up by 8 A.M., underneath a forty-foot cutout of Presley, when *Love Me Tender* premiered at the Paramount Theater in New York's Times Square. The Colonel gleefully worked the crowd, handing out "Elvis for President" buttons. A national release followed, in more theaters than any other film

Crowds gather around the Paramount Theater in Times Square, where the premiere of Love Me Tender *included a towering forty-foot cutout of Elvis Presley.*

in the history of the film's studio, 20th Century Fox. One fan in New Orleans watched it forty-two times in one week—after having already sat through forty-two showings of the previous week's movie so that she could see the coming attractions.

Elvis fled to Las Vegas to avoid the hoopla surrounding the premiere, where he began dating a Vegas show dancer named Dottie Harmony. The movie, meanwhile, got poor reviews but did terrific business at the box office. Around this time, the entertainment trade journal *Variety* declared that Presley was now, officially, a millionaire.

Loving You

Meanwhile, a new situation was beginning to brew: Elvis became eligible for military

service when, in October, the Memphis draft board had announced it was bringing up his file. Elvis spent the holidays at home with his parents and Dottie Harmony. They all accompanied him to a preinduction army physical in early 1957 before he returned to Hollywood for his second movie.

Originally entitled *Lonesome Cowboy* but renamed *Loving You* to reflect a song written expressly for it, the movie had a strong score and a good script based loosely on Elvis's own rags-to-riches story. He plays a small-town orphan who becomes an overnight sensation when signed to sing with a country band. *Loving You* marked the first attempts by Elvis and the Colonel to turn the singer into a mainstream entertainer who appealed to the whole family, rather than a one-shot wonder who would soon be forgotten.

Before shooting began, Elvis went into a Los Angeles recording studio. He

Frenzied young fans can barely contain their excitement as they watch the premiere of Elvis Presley's film Loving You.

recorded material for an upcoming religious album, songs that would be in the movie, and an Otis Blackwell composition, "All Shook Up," as his next single. Musically, he was doing fantastically well: his last release, "I Love You Too Much," was his eighth million-seller in under a year.

The mood on the movie set was relaxed and friendly. Wallis treated his star with respect and affection, and when Elvis's parents arrived for a visit, director Hal Kanter suggested making them extras. In the movie's climactic concert scene, Gladys and Vernon can be seen briefly as part of the audience.

The elder Presleys returned home in mid-March, and their son joined them briefly before beginning his third movie.

Electricity Bounced off Walls

Screenwriter Allen Weiss, in Guralnick's Last Train to Memphis, *describes the change when, during Presley's screen test, he was asked to read lines (which he did stiffly) and then mime singing.*

"The transformation was incredible . . . electricity bounced off the walls of the soundstage. One felt it as an awesome thing—like an earthquake in progress, only without the implicit threat. Watching this insecure country boy, who apologized when he asked for a rehearsal as though he had done something wrong, turn into absolute dynamite when he stepped into the bright lights and started lip synching the words of his familiar hit. He believed in it, and he made you believe it, no matter how 'sophisticated' your musical tastes were."

Gladys and Vernon started shopping for a house bigger than their home on Audubon. The neighbors there had never been kind to the Presleys—they disapproved of Gladys for keeping chickens in the yard and hanging her washing out. At one point, the neighbors had talked about buying the Presleys out; Elvis replied that *he* would buy the *neighbors* out. A Memphis newspaper, following up on this exchange, revealed that Elvis's house was the only one on the block that was completely paid for.

Eventually, Gladys and Vernon found a house they thought Elvis would like. Graceland had been built in 1939 on five hundred acres. The original owner, a doctor named Moore, had named it in honor of his aunt Grace. The property, south of downtown Memphis, had been gradually sold off over the years; only a little over thirteen acres remained when the Presleys saw it. But the mansion Dr. Moore had built was lovely, and the remaining land was more than adequate.

When the Presleys sold their old house, they turned down an offer from a bubble gum manufacturer who wanted to chop up its wood paneling and include small pieces with packs of gum. Elvis bought Graceland for $102,500, then paid as much again for a decorator to renovate it. The new furnishings included an eight-foot-square bed for Elvis, a fifteen-foot sofa, a soda fountain, and a chicken coop and swimming pool in the backyard.

Elvis loved the new house, and it was his main residence for the rest of his life. Just now he didn't have much time to enjoy it, however. He was needed back in Hollywood, where filming for *Jailhouse Rock* was about to start.

Elvis spent nearly $100,000 to remodel Graceland, his lavish estate in Memphis. Here, Elvis proudly stands beside a new gate that includes wrought iron caricatures of himself.

Jailhouse Rock

Leiber and Stoller, who had written "Hound Dog," composed virtually all the tunes for the new movie. They had maintained a successful career path before Elvis, writing hits for the Coasters and other groups. They were unimpressed with the singer and arrogant about their own abilities, but Elvis stunned them in *Jailhouse Rock.* As Stoller put it, "We thought we were the only two white kids who knew anything about the blues, but he knew all *kinds* of stuff."[41] The duo became the unofficial producers of the movie's soundtrack, and their hip collection of songs held together better than the uninspired tunes Presley sang in other movies.

Many fans and critics consider Elvis's earlier movies superior to his later films, and most consider *Jailhouse Rock* the best of all. Besides the catchy score, it had a strong plot about a young laborer who accidentally kills a man in a fight and is sent to prison, then gets a break as a singer and becomes a star. Along the way he acquires a loyal friend from jail—and, of course, gets the girl.

Careful viewers can spot Scotty, Bill, and D. J. as Elvis's band in both *Loving You* and *Jailhouse Rock*—plus, in the latter, Mike Stoller making his screen debut as the band's piano player. During the dance sequence to the song "Jailhouse Rock," the star accidentally inhaled one of the porcelain caps on his teeth. It went into a lung and required an emergency operation that left Presley hoarse for a few days—a freak accident that eerily echoed one of the plot twists in the script.

By the time *Jailhouse Rock* premiered in July, the new single, "Teddy Bear," was

Elvis dances in a scene from his movie Jailhouse Rock. *D. J. Fontana (left) and Scotty Moore (right), members of Elvis's band, appear in the background.*

jousting for the number-one spot with Jerry Lee Lewis's volatile rocker, "Whole Lotta Shakin' Goin' On." The popularity of "Teddy Bear" resulted in thousands of teddy bears delivered to Graceland by Elvis fans. He kept a few and gave most of them to charity.

Around this time, Presley began generously donating his time and money for other good causes, a practice he maintained all his life. He had a checkup to raise public awareness about cancer, launched a Teens vs. Polio campaign, and took part in a benefit for a Memphis charity called the Goodwill Fund, sponsored by black radio station WDIA.

He had originally wanted to sing at the gala concert, which featured such stars as Ray Charles and B. B. King. But the Colonel decided he should not perform. He had to settle for a brief speaking appearance. When he came onstage at the end to great applause and asked the mostly black audience how they were doing, somebody in the crowd shouted for more. Elvis grinned, gave a little shake of his hips, and broke the place up.

Elvis's participation in this event, and in similar events through the years, firmly contradict a rumor that had spread among the black community in Memphis—that he was racist. Allegedly, he had once remarked, "The only thing a Negro can do for me is buy my records or shine my shoes."

According to different versions, he was supposed to have made this statement in Boston, which he had never visited, or on

---

"That Felt Good"

In Last Train to Memphis, *Peter Guralnick describes the way Presley worked in the recording studio— in this case, on "Don't Be Cruel."*

"Elvis had the song played back for him again and started working it out on the guitar while the others listened for the first time. Then he sketched out a rough arrangement on the piano, which he showed to [pianist] Shorty Long, who made notes on the lead sheet. By this time he had memorized the lyrics. Scotty tried out a couple of openings, and Elvis suggested that he leave a little more space and told D. J. [Fontana] to 'come in behind Scotty and slow it down a little'; then the Jordanaires worked out their arrangement, and after about twenty minutes they were ready for a run-through.

After a single rehearsal, [producer Steve] Sholes was ready to record, but Elvis wanted to rehearse some more, so they did. The song continued to evolve through twenty-eight takes. It took on a lilting, almost casual, off-hand kind of feel, as Scotty virtually sat out except at the beginning and the end, Gordon Stoker of the Jordanaires came to sing a duet with Elvis on the chorus, and D. J. laid Elvis' leather-covered guitar across his lap and played the back of it with a mallet, to get an additional snare effect. It was hardly a formulaic approach, and it was clearly one that left the [producer] baffled. When they finally got the sound that he was looking for, Elvis pronounced, 'That felt good.' "

TV news journalist Edward R. Murrow's show, on which he never appeared. When the rumor was rampant, the black-oriented magazine *Jet* sent a reporter to confront him on it. Elvis told the reporter, "I never said anything like that, and people who know me know I wouldn't have said it." The *Jet* reporter concluded, "To Elvis, people are people, regardless of race, color or creed."[42]

The Band Breaks Up

Things were not going well with Elvis's longtime collaborators. Scotty Moore and Bill Black were increasingly frustrated. Their appearances with Elvis accounted for only about half the year, since he was busy with his movie schedule. Also, they made little money: a hundred dollars a week when at home, two hundred on the road. All their traveling expenses came out of that pay. Scotty said, "I didn't expect to get rich on this, and I certainly don't begrudge him [Elvis] any of the success . . . but I did expect to do better than I have and to make a good living for my family."[43]

Moore's and Black's contracts with the Colonel kept them from earning more. They could not make product endorsements to bring in extra money, play with anyone else, or appear anywhere as a unit except with Elvis. Furthermore, they felt as though Elvis was not appreciating them enough or standing up for them in their fights with the Colonel.

Many critics feel they were also outpaced by Elvis musically. Black was especially frustrated by his difficulties in learning to play the electric bass, which

had only recently come into common use. One day, while trying to learn an especially tricky part, Black lost his temper. He slammed the bass down, slid it across the floor, and stormed out of the studio as the others watched in disbelief. Presley seemed to take the tantrum in stride, though. He laughed, picked up the bass, and played it himself.

That fall, Moore and Black had been promised studio time to record an instrumental album of their own. When the Colonel went back on his promise and Elvis didn't stand up for them, it was the last straw. They wrote a letter of resignation, which Fontana did not sign; he had come on as a salaried player and felt he had been treated fairly. Elvis was angry and hurt when he heard about it. He felt that if Scotty and Bill had come to him earlier, they could have worked something out. He offered them a raise, but Scotty said he would need $10,000 just to get out of debt.

When Scotty and Bill made their resignation public, Elvis replied with a statement to reporters wishing them good luck. "We started out together, and I didn't want to cut anyone out of anything. . . . These boys could have had a job with me as long as I was making a dime." Scotty replied to the press, "We're both pretty stubborn. I guess he can be stubborn longer because he's got more money."[44]

Drafted

The fall of 1957 was an unsettled period for Presley. His career was going unbelievably well, but the trouble with the band and his mother's increasingly poor health—she had been ill for some time and was drinking heavily—left him depressed. Also, the draft was hanging over his head.

If he had wanted it, Elvis could have had the armed forces make him a special

Elvis received his draft notice during the fall of 1957. Although he tried to appear unaffected by the draft, he worried that time in the military would ruin his career.

case. He could have fulfilled his duty by entertaining the troops, as many famous performers had done during the Second World War. The navy wanted to form a special Elvis company; the air force wanted him to tour recruiting centers. But the Colonel thought that it was important for Presley's regular-guy image to accept the same treatment as everyone else.

In public, Elvis kept his cool about the draft. When the notice came just before Christmas, he picked it up at the board offices and then casually dropped by Sun Studios, cheerfully saying, "Hey, I'm going in." He told reporters that he was ready to serve his country, that he was grateful for the chance to pay back everything that America had given him.

With friends, though, he was franker. He feared that the public wouldn't remember him when he got out and fretted that the Colonel should have arranged a special deal for him. His friends tried to take his mind off it, saying that the government wouldn't let him go—he earned too much and paid too many taxes. (The Colonel often told reporters that it was his "patriotic duty" to keep Elvis in the 90 percent tax bracket.) But the reassurances were of little use.

The night of his formal notification, Presley put his Christmas present for the Colonel, a little red sports car, in a rental truck. He then drove it to Parker's offices outside Nashville. By the time he got there, a group of reporters was waiting. One of them had Army fatigues for him to model for the cameras, and Elvis joked that he would be wearing the uniform for real very soon.

He was right. But his two-year hitch in the Army would not, as he had feared, ruin his career.

6 The Army Years

After all, when you take him out of the entertainment business, what have you got left? A truck-driver.

the head of the
Memphis draft board

Elvis died the day he went into the Army.

John Lennon

The draft board granted Presley's request for a delay so he could shoot his next film, *King Creole*. Shortly after his twenty-third birthday, he arrived in California with a large contingent of friends, bodyguards, and business associates.

He immediately began recording material for the film, with Leiber and Stoller (who contributed three songs to the movie) again in charge of production. But then the Colonel tried to browbeat Leiber, laid up in New York with pneumonia, to sign a blank contract ("Don't worry, we'll fill it in later"). Leiber refused, Stoller stood by his partner, and the Colonel dropped them from any future projects. The gifted songwriters, perhaps the best to write for Presley, never again worked directly with him.

King Creole was another strong dramatic vehicle, this one about a poor New Orleans waiter who gradually gets involved with mobsters. It was Elvis's favorite of all his movies, and the first to be filmed partly on location in Louisiana.

Filming, Fun, and Friends

One day in the studio cafeteria, Presley demonstrated that in some ways he was still a star-struck kid. While eating with Jan Shepard, who played his sister in the film, Elvis realized that his idol, Marlon Brando, was sitting behind him. Elvis was too shy to introduce himself, so Shepard told him to push his chair back—he'd bump into Brando. Presley did it, Brando stood up, and the two famous young men shook hands. Elvis was so excited that he told anyone who would listen that he couldn't believe it had really happened.

When shooting was over, Elvis returned to Memphis and crammed as much fun as possible into his remaining time. He saw movies, went roller-skating, organized football games with his pals, went shopping for cars and records. The night before his induction, he and his latest girlfriend, former beauty queen Anita Wood, went with some friends to a drive-in movie and stayed up all night.

Early the next morning, March 24, he arrived at the draft board with his parents

Elvis bids farewell to his parents, Vernon and Gladys, on the eve of his induction into the army.

and several carloads of friends. A couple of dozen reporters and photographers were already waiting in the light rain. Elvis told them he was very nervous. By 7:15 he was on a bus with twelve other inductees, headed to the Veterans Hospital for examinations and processing. The Colonel stood outside the hospital, handing out balloons advertising *King Creole.*

Fort Chaffee

When processing was over, the inductees boarded a bus for Fort Chaffee, Arkansas, 150 miles away. As his mother and father wept, Private Elvis Presley, serial number 53 310 761, called out to his girlfriend, "Goodbye, baby." To the limousine that had brought him, he called out, "Goodbye, you long black sonofabitch." Elvis was in the army now; he had gone from a monthly income of $100,000 to $78.

Despite Presley's publicly stated wish to be treated like any other soldier, the first days of army life were a circus. His slightest move was painstakingly recorded for a curious public. Some 100 civilians and 50 newsmen, plus 200 dependents of military personnel, were waiting at Fort Chaffee. Dozens of photographers surrounded Elvis at every turn. One even tried to hide in the barracks to get a snapshot of him in bed.

After a few hours of sleep, the new recruits were up at 5:30, only to endure the newsmen—and the Colonel—tagging along for breakfast, five hours of tests and a series of lectures. When a reporter asked what he'd do with the seven dollars in partial pay he received, Elvis smiled and said he would start a loan company. Presley also said his barracks mates were treating him as well as any other new recruit. "They've been swell to me. . . . They consider themselves for what they are—just GIs—the same as me. That's the way I want it."[45]

Then came another ritual for any new soldier: the haircut. Elvis's trim was surely the most-photographed and most-written-about haircut in history. He smiled for the

it took twenty-five minutes for someone to recognize him. A small riot ensued, and the waitresses were fighting over his chair as the soldiers fought their way out. Elvis made up for the fuss by buying cigarettes and candy for everyone.

At Fort Hood, newsmen were allowed in for one day, and then Private Presley was strictly off-limits. This allowed him to get on with being a soldier, which he did quite competently; soon he had been awarded a marksman medal and a sharpshooter medal, and was named acting assistant squad leader.

Given the standard two weeks' leave after two months of training, he went eagerly back to Graceland and his family. He told reporters he was happy to eat his mother's cooking again: "I've eaten things

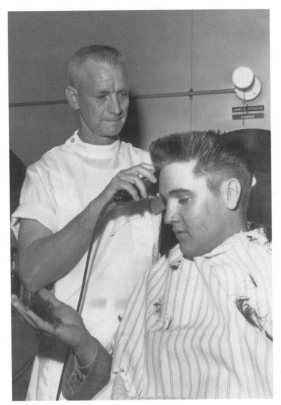

Elvis holds a handful of hair while an army barber trims his famous locks.

fifty-five newsmen surrounding him and, as his famous locks fell to the floor, muttered, "Hair today, gone tomorrow." A special detail of soldiers swept up the hair and destroyed it to keep it away from fans.

Basic Training

Presley was assigned to the Second Armored Division at Fort Hood, outside Killeen, Texas. He traveled there by bus, bypassing the usual stops because of the crowds. When his bus stopped at a restaurant in Hillsboro, Texas, two big soldiers were assigned to sit on either side of him;

Private Elvis Presley, a new recruit in the U.S. Army, undergoes basic training.

in the Army that I never ate before, and I've eaten things that I didn't know what it was, but after a hard day of basic training, you could eat a rattlesnake."[46]

While in Memphis he wore his uniform because he was proud of it. RCA released the first of Elvis's greatest-hits LPs and his twenty-second single, "Wear My Ring Around Your Neck." And *King Creole* opened to excellent reviews. Even the normally disdainful *New York Times* liked it: "As the lad himself might say, cut my legs off and call me Shorty! Elvis Presley can act."[47]

Steve Sholes had arranged for a last recording session in Nashville, which produced five good takes—giving RCA a total of nine Elvis songs ready for release. This date, Elvis's last for nearly two years, was also his first session without Scotty and Bill; the band was composed of guitarists Hank Garland and Chet Atkins, Bob Moore on bass, pianist Floyd Cramer, Buddy Harmon on drums, and the Jordanaires.

Elvis Presley, on leave from the army to visit his ailing mother, walks down the corridor of Baptist Memorial Hospital with his father.

The Death of Gladys

Colonel Parker had discovered that soldiers could live off base if they had legal dependents, which Vernon and Gladys were. Elvis was eager to live with his parents in their own house, rather than in the crowded barracks. So he and the elder Presleys, plus Minnie Mae, Vernon's mother, moved to a rented house in Killeen, near the base. Elvis spent his evenings there and often traveled on weekend leaves to see friends in Waco.

But Gladys was increasingly ill. The problem was twofold: a weak heart and hepatitis, a serious liver disease. Both were aggravated by long-term abuse of diet pills and alcohol. On August 8 Vernon took Gladys to Memphis for tests, but she collapsed at home and was admitted to Baptist Memorial Hospital.

When Elvis asked for leave to go see her, his commanding officer at first was reluctant to let him go. He worried that the press would accuse him of granting special privileges. But Gladys's doctor insisted, and late on August 12 Presley arrived at the hospital.

Vernon was sleeping on a cot next to her bed. Elvis spent the night and the whole next day there as well, finally leaving at midnight to get some sleep at home. But then, at 3:30 A.M. on August 14, he was awakened by a phone call. She had taken a turn for the worse. By the time Elvis got there, his mother was dead.

A Grieving Son

Jane and Michael Stern, in Elvis World, *describe Presley's grief over his dead mother.*

"He threw himself on her coffin, weeping over her tiny feet, calling her by the baby-talk names they had used in private conversation. He caressed her lifeless body, combing its hair, wailing laments as he clutched her pink housecoat (the one he had given her) to his chest. He talked to the corpse, telling it which visitors had come to pay their respects. No one, no relatives or friends, not even his father, could penetrate the delirium that engulfed Elvis. . . .

'I lived my whole life for you!' he cried out at the cemetery. 'Everything I have is gone,' he moaned as he fell upon the casket. . . . He grieved like he sang—racked with emotion, oblivious to the judgments of others.

What a surreal vision of hell it must have been for Elvis. His mother—the one woman who knew how to comfort him—was gone; but legions of would-be Gladyses—fans who wanted fiercely to mother him—swarmed the cemetery and Graceland gates, fighting to be by his side.

What did they know about his real fears? About the nightmares and sleepwalking and insomnia that had haunted him since childhood? The boy who never left home in all his twenty-three years could now never go home. For hours, he stood outside Graceland looking up at the white-columned porch of the dream house he had bought for his mother. He spent nine days locked in his bedroom while the world waited, camera ready."

On their knees beside the bed, weeping openly, Elvis and his father waited until the hearse arrived to take her away and then went home. By the time reporters found them at Graceland, they were sitting on the steps with their arms around each other. "She's all we lived for," Elvis told them. "She was always my best girl."[48]

Hundreds of well-wishers had gathered at the Graceland gates by the time her body was brought to the house. Telegrams and letters of condolence—over one hundred thousand in all—began arriving. Gladys's body was moved the next day to a funeral home, where thousands came to pay their respects.

Elvis was inconsolable for weeks. His leave was extended, but finally he had to return to Fort Hood. Before he left, he left instructions that nothing in his mother's room was to be changed. He even ordered that the pane of glass she had fallen against when she collapsed was not to be repaired.

Gradually, Presley had to pull himself together and get on with his life. He had received word that in September he and fourteen hundred other soldiers were sailing for duty in West Germany. The 1950s were a time of great tension between the Western powers and Communist East Germany, and there was constant fear that East Germany might launch an invasion to the west. The American military was a forceful presence in West Germany, and Presley's tank unit would be part of it.

To Germany

Late that year, Private Presley traveled by train to New York to board his ship for Germany. The scene awaiting him at the Brooklyn Army Terminal was riotous. Over a hundred newsmen, a squad of RCA executives, Vernon, Anita, the Colonel, and dozens of others were assembled for a giant, hour-long press conference.

He finally was able to march up the ship's gangplank, waving and carrying a duffle bag. The band played "Tutti Frutti," thousands on shore screamed, and cameras snapped. He had to walk up the gangplank eight times before the newsmen were satisfied. On board, he recorded a Christmas message for his fans, which, together with an edited version of the press conference, the Colonel issued on record as "Elvis Sails!"

On deck, Elvis handed out souvenir postcards and pictures and threw kisses to shore. When he playfully buckled his

knees and snapped his fingers, the crowd erupted. And then he was gone. As the *New York Herald-Tribune* put it, "His admirers shrieked. Colonel Parker beamed. The Department of Defense man from Washington who had overseen the operation wiped his brow and sighed."[49]

In Germany

Elvis records were already big sellers in Germany, and a crowd of five hundred was waiting for him when his ship landed in Bremerhaven on October 1. But Presley was hustled onto a train and taken to his post outside Friedberg, a small town in central Germany. The base officers held a

Private Elvis Presley waves goodbye to his fans as he boards an army transport ship destined for Germany.

three-day "open house" for crowds of reporters, then declared their famous charge off-limits.

He was assigned to be a scout jeep driver. Scouts were needed to travel the countryside by jeep and provide information on road conditions, so that if an invasion did occur, Western tanks would not find themselves trapped by unusable roads.

Private Presley was a model soldier. Since he was still allowed to live off base with his dependents, his father and grandmother joined him in a modest, middle-class home near the base. Usually, he was awake at 5:00 or 5:30 in the morning and not home again until 5:00 P.M. or later. A sign outside his house read: "Autographs between 7:30 and 8:30 P.M."

The army didn't affect Elvis's earnings or popularity as badly as he had feared. Elvis earned two million dollars for the year 1958, though he had been a soldier almost the entire time. He got ten thousand letters a week, some of them marked simply "Elvis, U.S. Army." Still, RCA was worried about the scarcity of new material, and what remained had been carefully doled out. By February 1959, the unreleased material was getting thin: there were no Presley songs on *Billboard*'s "Hot 100" for the first time in almost three years.

In March 1959, the company issued "A Fool Such as I," his nineteenth consecutive million-seller. The last of the unreleased material, "A Big Hunk o' Love," came out in June—the same month Presley was promoted to specialist fourth class. To make up for the lack of new material, RCA repackaged old songs and found that they sold nearly as well.

In August Colonel Parker announced that Presley's first post-army film would be about—surprise!—an army tank sergeant stationed in Germany. It was to be called *G.I. Blues*, and it would again team Elvis with producer Hal Wallis.

The money was rolling in, but not fast enough; everyone was eager for Elvis to

Upon his arrival in Germany, Elvis was stationed at a base outside the small town of Friedberg. Base officers held a three-day "open house" so that the public and media could visit the famous soldier.

get out. Near the end of the wait, the Colonel had a fake newspaper printed up. A huge banner headline read ELVIS RE-ENLISTS; underneath it was a smaller headline, WALLIS COLLAPSES. The Colonel wrapped it around Wallis's paper in Los Angeles and left it on the producer's front steps one morning. Wallis read the main headline and really did collapse before he got around to looking at the smaller headline.

Out at Last

Life in the army was mostly routine, but not everything was dreary. Elvis became interested in karate and worked his way up to a second-degree black belt. He also met a very special girl: Priscilla Beaulieu, the fourteen-year-old daughter of an air force officer. They began dating regularly. In time, Elvis would become as obsessed with Priscilla as he had once been with his mother.

In early 1960 Presley was promoted to sergeant and began commanding a three-man reconnaissance team. Then came news that he would be discharged in February, a month early. The media immediately snapped into action: there were magazine contests, special radio programs, and a rerelease of *Jailhouse Rock*. Plans were made to press a million copies of his first post-army single before it was even recorded. And it was announced that Elvis's first public appearance on a Frank Sinatra television special would earn him $125,000—more than any other TV guest had ever received.

The day before he left Germany, he took part in another huge press conference. The big surprise there was the presence of Marion Keisker, his old friend

Priscilla Beaulieu waves goodbye as Elvis Presley departs Germany in February 1960. Priscilla, the daughter of an air force officer, started dating Elvis when she was just fourteen years old.

from Sun Records and one of the people most responsible for bringing Elvis to public attention.

Keisker was now a captain in the air force, assigned to the Armed Forces Television network in Germany. When they met, Keisker said, "Hi, hon." Elvis was astonished: he cried, "Marion! In Germany! And an officer! What do I do? Kiss you or salute you?" She replied, "In that order."[50] The officer in charge of the proceedings was disturbed by this lack of respect for a superior officer; Elvis explained that if Keisker had not thought to make an extra tape recording one day in Memphis, none of them would have been there.

Priscilla saw Elvis off at the Frankfurt airport. He landed at Fort Dix, New Jersey, to find a snowstorm and, of course, a gang of newsmen. After yet another huge press conference (during which Elvis's casual remark that he probably would grow his sideburns back sent reporters sprinting for the phones), Presley was formally discharged.

He had done his service to his country and was once again a civilian. Now it remained to be seen whether he could resume his sidetracked career.

Chapter

7 The Movie Years

They [Elvis movies] all have two things in common: none lost money, and none is [connected with] reality.

writer Stanley Booth

They don't need titles. They could be numbered. They would still sell.

MGM executive who worked
on five of Elvis's movies

The music scene had changed while Presley was in the army. For one thing, several rivals were gone. Jerry Lee Lewis, who had lost his rock 'n' roll audience because of a scandalous marriage to his fourteen-year-old cousin, was banished to the wilds of the country charts. Little Richard had temporarily given up music to become a minister. Buddy Holly and Ritchie Valens were dead, victims of a plane crash.

Another scandal, involving payola—money and favors given to disc jockeys by record companies—had rocked the music industry. One of the hardest hit was Alan Freed, the influential disc jockey who probably coined the phrase "rock and roll." Because of the scandal, the industry and fans alike were wary.

In addition, public taste had changed: the big sellers were now tame singers like Ricky Nelson, Fabian, and Bobby Darin. This shift away from the biting rock and roll pioneered by Elvis was another element of uncertainty. None of the new singers was a serious threat, however; no one had come along during Elvis's absence who seemed likely to take his throne.

Soon after returning home, Presley went to Nashville for his first recording session in two years. The date produced "Stuck on You," the song with a million advance orders. The next day, he took a train to Miami to tape a TV special hosted by Frank Sinatra. The trip was like a combination presidential whistle-stop tour and royal procession. Scotty Moore, who was along for the ride, remembered, "In every little town along the way the tracks were lined. Twenty-four hours a day. The whole trip. Photographers. Cameramen. Kids. I don't know where they came from."[51]

The Sinatra show, viewed from today's perspective, is a fascinating bit of history—the meeting of two different idols from two different generations. In the 1940s, as a skinny, bow-tied crooner, Frank Sinatra had evoked nearly as sensational a reaction from young female fans as Elvis. By 1957, Sinatra was a member of the musical establishment. He disapproved of rock and roll, calling it "phony and false, and sung, written, and played for the most part by cretinous goons."[52]

Frank Sinatra (left) and Elvis Presley (right) team up for duet of "Love Me Tender" during Sinatra's TV special. Elvis was paid an astronomical fee of $125,000 for his six-minute appearance.

Then it was on to Hollywood for *G.I. Blues.* The movie's plot was simple: Elvis plays a tank gunner in Germany out to win a bet that he can get a date with a nightclub dancer, singing eleven songs along the way. *G.I. Blues* was a big step in Parker's plan to move his client away from rock and roll. Most of the songs were bland pop tunes, and even the version of "Blue Suede Shoes" that Elvis sings in it is weak compared with the earlier recording.

The film got generally poor reviews. Typical was the reaction of one movie-industry newspaper, the *Hollywood Reporter.* "When they took the boy out of the country, they apparently took the country out of the boy. It is a subdued and changed Elvis Presley who has returned from military service in Germany to star in Hal Wallis's *G.I. Blues.*" The review concluded that the picture would "have to depend on the loyalty of Presley fans to bail it out at the box office."[53] That it did—the film was a smash.

Big Changes

Meanwhile, big changes were taking place in Elvis's personal life. His father married Dee Stanley, a woman he had met in Germany, and moved into a house down the street from Graceland. Elvis, still respectful of his mother's memory, was extremely upset. He saw the second marriage as a mark of disrespect toward Gladys, and he refused to attend the wedding.

Vernon and Gladys were gone, and—although his grandmother and an aunt continued to live with him at Graceland—for virtually the first time in his life Elvis did not live with either parent. Soon, how-

But Sinatra wanted high ratings for his special, so Colonel Parker negotiated a $125,000 fee for six minutes of Presley's time. Elvis sang one of Sinatra's signature tunes, "Witchcraft," and together they sang "Love Me Tender." The two famous singers sounded terrific, both separately and together. When the program aired on May 12, Sinatra got his desired huge ratings and Elvis received another sign that all was well.

Back in Nashville, Elvis returned to the studio and knocked out twelve songs in twelve hours. The resulting LP was released a week later as *Elvis Is Back,* and it shot to number one.

ever, someone else moved in who would become equally important.

Since his return, Elvis had invited Priscilla to visit Graceland for extended vacations. Her parents were reluctant at first, but Elvis was able to persuade them to accept the unusual arrangement. Presley pointed out that his family would act as Priscilla's chaperons. Eventually, Priscilla moved in permanently to her own suite of rooms at Graceland.

Presley openly worshiped Priscilla, and he did everything possible to give her what she wanted. He enrolled her in a private girl's high school, from which she graduated in 1963. He also sent her to a finishing school, gave her modeling and dancing classes, and let her buy anything she wanted. She even began resembling Elvis; her cascade of jet-black hair, makeup, and even facial features began to look eerily like his.

Meanwhile, Elvis had relationships with several other women in Los Angeles, Las Vegas, and Memphis. Priscilla was being groomed for marriage, and until then she was off-limits.

Girls! Girls! Girls!

Presley received several Grammies in 1961, for "Are You Lonesome Tonight?" and the *G.I. Blues* LP, and he picked up another stack of gold records, each representing a million-selling disc. He recorded an LP of spirituals, *His Hand in Mine*; it did not sell massively, but it was a labor of love and Elvis was happy with it. He also sang at a benefit concert in Hawaii; it would be his last public performance until 1968. While in the islands Elvis shot his next film, *Blue Hawaii*, a light comedy in

Merely Awful

Not everyone was pleased to see Elvis out of the army. As quoted in Jerry Hopkins's Elvis, *critic John Shanley in the* New York Times *was rough on the returning hero.*

"The recent liberation from the Army of Elvis Presley may have been one of the most irritating events since the invention of itching powder. While he was in the service he lost his sideburns, drove a truck and apparently behaved in an acceptable military manner. But now he is free to perform in public again, as he did on last night's 'Frank Sinatra Show' on Channel 7. Accompanied by an orchestra and the shrieks of a group of his frenzied young admirers, he did several numbers including a duet with Mr. Sinatra. Although Elvis became a sergeant in the Army, as a singer he never left the awkward squad. There was nothing morally reprehensible about his performance, it was merely awful."

which he plays the musical son of a wealthy plantation owner.

Most of Elvis's post-army movies are silly, bubbleheaded, sexist, and sometimes amazingly bad. But they also have a sunny, innocent charm that is great fun to watch. Above all, they are harmless—quite a change from Elvis's first impact on America, when he projected an image of dangerous rebellion. As the *New York Times* once put it, "Music, youth and customs were much changed by Elvis Presley twelve years ago; from the twenty-six movies he has made since he sang 'Heartbreak Hotel,' you would never guess it."[54]

The general tone of an Elvis movie can be summed up by promotional ad lines like, "Watch Elvis sing and swing and give the bikini-clad beauties and the girl-happy guys a rompin', rockin' good time!" Or by the song titles: "(There's) No Room to Rhumba in a Sports Car," "Song of the Shrimp," "Do the Clam," "Fort Lauderdale Chamber of Commerce." Every one of his movies, even the worst, was a smash hit; his faithful fans came in droves to see him no matter how terrible the film. And they made Elvis the highest paid entertainer in history; his usual fee was a million dollars plus 50 percent of the profits, an astronomical sum by the standards of the day.

The movies came fast and furious. He was a Florida hillbilly in *Follow That Dream*, a boxer in *Kid Galahad*, a boat captain in *Girls! Girls! Girls!*. *It Happened at the Fair*, set at the 1962 Seattle World's Fair, includes in a bit part a kid actor, Kurt Russell, who would one day play Elvis in a TV docudrama.

Other roles included *Fun in Acapulco* (trapeze artist–lifeguard), *Kissin' Cousins* (a good guy–bad guy double role), *Roustabout* (a carnival worker), and *Tickle*

Me (singing cowboy on a dude ranch). In *Harum Scarum*, Elvis plays an American movie star who gets kidnapped in a mythical Arab country; he runs around in white robes and somehow ends up in Las Vegas. About *Frankie and Johnny* (Elvis as a riverboat gambler), the *New York Times* commented, "Even compared to some previous Presley turkeys, this one almost sheds feathers from the start."[55]

An early promotional ad for the movie Spin-Out *includes dancing girls, a sports car, and Elvis—the star of the production.*

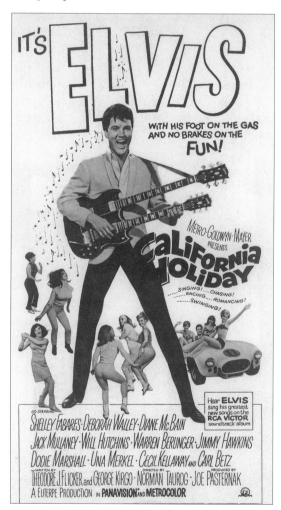

Elvis Presley and his bride, Priscilla, were wed at the Aladdin Hotel in Las Vegas in April 1967.

The King's Wedding

After years of speculation in the gossip columns, Priscilla and Elvis finally married in late April 1967. Like everything surrounding Elvis by now, the Las Vegas wedding was kept secret until the last possible moment. And like everything surrounding Elvis by now, it was also noisy, expensive, and garish.

Media associates and friends of the Colonel's received telegrams asking them to fly to Vegas with photographers who could be trusted. Meanwhile, Elvis and Priscilla arrived there in the dead of night. They went straight to the Clark County courthouse, kept open especially for them; Elvis paid fifteen dollars for a marriage license. The couple proceeded to the Aladdin Hotel, where they greeted Priscilla's parents and Vernon and went off to separate suites to rest and get ready.

That morning, invited newsmen were allowed in the Aladdin. Scores of others were left milling around. Nothing had been officially announced, but the word was out.

Elvis and Priscilla were wed that morning in a suite of the hotel. The ceremony, performed by a Nevada Supreme Court judge, lasted eight minutes. Elvis was dressed in black; Priscilla wore white chiffon and satin with a six-foot train. Her ring had a three-carat diamond and twenty smaller ones. Elvis's friends Joe Esposito and Marty Lacker were the best men; Priscilla's sister Michelle was the maid of honor.

Afterward, a reception was held that featured a five-foot cake, breakfast for a hundred, and a strolling string trio. Following the inevitable press conference, the newlyweds left for a four-day honeymoon in Palm Springs. Then it was home to Graceland and the Circle G Ranch, a

Remodeling Graceland

Jane and Michael Stern, in Elvis World, *have this to say about the excesses of the remodeling Elvis undertook at Graceland.*

"Understatement, subtlety, clarity, harmony, integrity of materials, comfort: forget those decorating clichés! With a thoroughness never achieved in his nastiest rock-and-roll songs or in his loudest Las Vegas costumes, Elvis has here designed the ultimate challenge to convention, uncensored by any designer's notion of what is appropriate.

'Good taste,' 'bad taste,' 'kitsch' [tacky pop]: such small terms do not do justice to Graceland. This house is too far out to be circumscribed. It is a black hole in the aesthetic universe, where ordinary standards vanish. . . . You have seen this place before, but not in the real world. . . .

One is reminded of how facile Elvis was as a singer, able to slide from low-down blues to ballads or to sing sacred music with unholy ardor [passion]. Likewise, he was too restless to have Graceland conform to a single motif. How drab that would have been! How much more fun to have every kind of way-out room you could think of, all in one big house."

163-acre spread just over the Mississippi state line that Elvis had recently bought.

Married Life

When Elvis settled in with Priscilla, he was forced to give up many of his bachelor habits. For one thing, Priscilla didn't like the Memphis Mafia.

"Memphis Mafia" was the name the press had given to the guys who regularly hung out with Elvis. At any given time, anywhere from seven to twelve men were on Elvis's payroll. They included old high school chums like George Klein, Red West, and Sonny West, family members like his step-brother Dave Stanley, and friends picked up along the road to fame, like army buddy Charlie Hodge.

Officially they were bodyguards, chauffeurs, or valets. Their real jobs, though, were to shelter Elvis and keep him entertained. They were fanatically loyal to Elvis, protected him from any unwanted unpleasantness, and catered to his every whim. Whatever "E" wanted, "E" got.

They were experts at judging Presley's mood and knowing what was needed to make him happy. They might play touch football. They might organize a party with lots of attractive girls. They might stage a water-balloon fight on the set of Elvis's latest movie. Or they might go riding in a pack on motorcycles, a routine that got them dubbed "El's Angels" by the press.

To Elvis, the group was just a bunch of good old boys he felt comfortable around—they thought like he did and liked what he did, unlike other people he might encounter in the music industry. Of course, they were also being paid to think like him and like the same things. He hated being by himself, and wanted people he liked and trusted to be around him constantly.

To Priscilla, however, the Memphis Mafia were nothing more than freeloading yes-men. She thought they were taking cruel advantage of Elvis. At her insistence, Elvis fired some of them and kept others at a distance. This lasted for a few years, although gradually several worked their way back onto the payroll.

Elvis also gave in to Priscilla's request for a Los Angeles home. Previously, when making a movie in Hollywood, he and the Memphis Mafia had always rented houses. But Priscilla wanted a place of her own. The house they chose, at 1174 Hillcrest Road, was an ornate mansion with four huge bedrooms, six baths, a pool, and a sweeping view.

Elvis loved being married. He couldn't stop talking about how happy he was. Then, while shooting *Speedway*, Priscilla told him she was pregnant.

Presley was even more delighted. More than anything, he wanted a family. Actor Bill Bixby, who was shooting *Speedway* with him, recalled, "Elvis was happier than I had seen him. . . . He seemed totally content. I remember him whistling and humming. He was thinner and everything

seemed to be falling into place."[56] On February 1, 1968, nine months after the wedding, Lisa Marie Presley was born. The Presleys were jubilant, and Colonel Parker announced to the press that he had already drawn up a contract—since the new arrival would no doubt one day be a singer.

A New Revolution

In some ways, Presley was doing unbelievably well. In 1965, the year he celebrated his thirtieth birthday and the year he and the Colonel celebrated their tenth anniversary together, the seventeen films

Elvis Presley prepares to take his wife, Priscilla, and their newborn daughter, Lisa Marie, home from Baptist Memorial Hospital. Lisa Marie, their only child, was born on February 1, 1968.

they had released so far had grossed about $130 million; the hundred million records they had sold had made them another $150 million.

But in some ways he was slipping. Despite a steady string of releases, Elvis's last number-one hit had been "Good Luck Charm" in the spring of 1962. For years he had been making insipid recordings, with no strong musical hand to help him shape his sound, as Sam Phillips and Steve Sholes had once done. He was relying on the loyalty of his fans to keep sales up.

Meanwhile, the number-one song in America for 1965 was "I Feel Fine" by a group from England called the Beatles. A new revolution in popular music, the British Invasion, had been under way since 1963.

The leaders of the invasion, the Beatles, were as charismatic as Elvis—and gifted composers as well. The Beatles and other top invasion groups (including the Yardbirds, the Rolling Stones, and the Animals) made music heavily influenced by American blues and R&B. They reminded fans of the exciting promise Elvis had once held out—of strong, vibrant music that really mattered. The British Invasion took America by storm and posed the first real threat to Presley's supremacy of the music charts.

Presley saw that he needed a new direction, but taking one was not easy. For one thing, the Colonel encouraged him to record only safe, dull material. Parker knew that any old junk would sell, and that middle-of-the-road music appealed to more listeners than more challenging music would. The Colonel was convinced that the Beatles were a passing fad, and he put pressure on Elvis to stay where he was.

Also, Presley's producers and backup musicians were by now changing with nearly every session. He was denied the kind of supportive environment enjoyed

During the 1960s, the Beatles led a revolution in music known as the British Invasion. Their strong, vibrant sound was heavily influenced by American blues and R&B.

In Elvis, *Dave Marsh comments on the songs Elvis sang in the movies.*

"Who could sing such drool and make it stick? Who could put across such drivel and keep the customers lined up for more?

Only Elvis. But Elvis was not content with carny tricks. He took the miracle to its extreme; he seized each song that possessed a glimmer of worth and wrung out its full potential. The catch is that Elvis sang the hell out of even these ridiculously titled songs. They remain lousy songs—but his performances are anything but."

by other singers of the era, such as those at Motown Records. Motown singers like Stevie Wonder, Marvin Gaye, and Diana Ross were part of tight-knit teams, along with their producers and writers, whose members depended heavily on each other for creative inspiration.

Finally, Presley was hampered by his not being a songwriter. Many of the best new performers—John Lennon and Paul McCartney, Mick Jagger and Keith Richards, Bob Dylan, Smokey Robinson—sang their own material. Elvis could not.

Often the credits on his records claim that he cowrote the tunes, but this was a ruse on the part of the Colonel to get extra money from royalties. He would tell songwriters that if they wanted Elvis to record their songs, they would have to surrender half of the royalty money. Some songwriters refused to do this, although many were satisfied with the arrangement. As Bumps Blackwell, who wrote several Presley hits, put it, "Fifty percent of several million records is much tastier than a hundred percent of zero."[57]

Too often, the ones who did go along with the Colonel's arrangement were mediocre craftsmen who produced dull material. As a result, the best tunes were often unavailable, and the ones that were available were often flat and lifeless.

Elvis had become part of the establishment. Once the idol of every musician, he was now a holdover from a previous era—the opposite of what musicians like the Beatles wanted to be. As critic Dave Marsh put it, "They [the new musicians] said this with respect—Elvis had, in his way, given them their start after all—but they said it firmly. Elvis had mapped out not only the route to success but also its most significant and deadly pitfalls."[58]

Changing Gears

Throughout the mid-sixties, Presley began to rebel against this stagnation. For years he had been passive. He had naively accepted the Colonel's actions as being all

The $25,000 Watch

In Hopkins's Elvis, *DJ Ron Jacobs describes seeing the Colonel in action on the set of* Blue Hawaii.

"There had to be fifty-seven technicians and directors and script girls and makeup men and all the rest standing around with reflectors, waiting for the clouds to clear so the light would be just right for a matching shot. Finally the sun comes out and they have twenty-six seconds to shoot. Elvis is ready. Everybody is ready. The director calls action and Parker comes out of the bushes, on camera, screaming for Hal Wallis. Wallis comes rushing up. The shot's been blown. He's furious, but he's trying to keep control, even if his face is purple. He asks Parker what's wrong and Parker says Elvis is wearing his own gold watch in the shot and the contract doesn't call for his providing wardrobe, but that's okay, so long as they come up with an additional $25,000 for the use of the watch."

for the best. He seemed to care little about which movies he made or which songs he recorded. But as the entertainment industry changed, Elvis sensed that he needed to change too.

He started with the movies. *Stay Away Joe* marked a beginning in this shift. It was a western with a more serious script than most Presley films—and only three songs. Presley hoped it would help him fulfill his ambition of becoming a serious actor.

Elvis also slowly changed his way of making records. He hooked up with a sympathetic producer, Nashville veteran Felton Jarvis. Jarvis had recorded Presley's Grammy-winning collection of spirituals, *How Great Thou Art.* Together, they began tightening Presley's sound and searching out more interesting songs, like Jimmy Reed's "Big Boss Man" and Jerry Reed's "Guitar Man." When these tunes were released in late 1967, they were Elvis's biggest hits in recent memory—they didn't reach even the Top Ten, but they were still stronger than anything he'd done in a long time.

Then, in early 1968, the Colonel announced plans for an Elvis Christmas special—the first appearance on TV by the singer since 1960, and the first time Elvis had been in front of a live audience in years. NBC would pay him a half million dollars, but the show's aftermath would prove to be more important than the money. The "Comeback Special," as it came to be known, would prove to the world that Elvis Presley was still the King of Rock and Roll.

8 Comeback

There is something magical about watching a man who has lost himself find his way back home.

critic Jon Landau on the 1968 "Comeback Special"

If it had been up to the Colonel, the Christmas special would have been a no-brainer: a bunch of traditional carols and songs, a few words of yuletide greetings, and his client could have walked away with half a million dollars. As writer Dave Marsh put it, it was "exactly what any anonymous TV hack would have done, only less of it and for a higher price. This was Parker's dream of holiday bliss."[59]

For once, however, Parker did not get his way. Elvis felt that a strong return to live performance would renew him both personally and professionally. The man hired to put the special together, producer Steve Binder, also felt strongly about involving Presley again in the creative process. Binder and Parker fought from the very beginning over the show's creative control, and for once Parker lost.

The turning point came when Binder convinced Presley that his popularity was slipping. One day, the producer took Elvis on a stroll along Sunset Strip in Los Angeles. Elvis was reluctant; he hadn't been out in daylight and in public in over a decade.

But then Presley, Binder, and a couple of the Memphis Mafia spent fifteen minutes hanging around outside a strip bar in midday—and no one noticed. Even after Elvis began acting like a clown to try and draw attention, he was ignored.

The lesson was not lost on Presley. He had been isolated too long. He hated the idea that he wasn't popular anymore, and he couldn't bear the thought of being anonymous. As Dave Marsh put it, "Binder got more than just [Presley's] cooperation when he suggested that stroll on the Strip. . . . He got an Elvis Presley who was determined, once again, to go out there and *show 'em.*"[60] After that, despite the Colonel's objections, Binder was allowed free rein to create his show.

The Triumph

As the program was taped that summer, Presley was terrified that people would laugh at him onstage. It had been so long since he'd performed. But he held in all his frustration and turned it into performance energy. The show's music producer, Bones Howe, recalled, "He was so frightened when he went out [onstage] and so with it once he got there. . . . He

Elvis charms the audience during his Christmas 1968 TV special. The "Comeback Special" was a tremendous success that reestablished Elvis as the King of Rock and Roll.

came off the stage, we practically had to carry him off. We were slapping each other on the back. It was like we'd won a football game."[61]

When the program aired on December 3, 1968, it was clear from the first moment that the star was in control. Elvis was thinner even than in the fifties, and dressed in a tight black leather suit. His eyes were full of fire, his dangerously charming grin was in place, and his hair was perfect. As Dave Marsh commented, "He was not only the Elvis of everyone's dreams, he was actually a little bit better. . . . [H]e had that gaze in his eyes again, the one that said he was ready to conquer the universe, perish the cost."[62]

The show's structure alternated straight musical numbers with semidramatic sequences of music and dance. Together, they told a loose story about a young man seeking adventure and fortune. The staged dance sequences (including a controversial one set in a house of prostitution) seem corny today, but they are the only part of the show that has aged poorly. The material was strong, dating from the Sun days to the best of the new songs. The singer's voice had deepened and lowered over the years; the high, lonesome ache of the Sun records was replaced by a confident new voice that was especially effective with ballads.

There was only one real holiday song, the soulful "Blue Christmas," put there to please the Colonel. The show's final tune was as close to a "message" song as Presley had ever performed: the hymnlike ballad "If I Can Dream," composed for the occasion by the show's choral director, Earl Brown. As Dave Marsh has pointed out, it was the perfect ending, one that described Elvis's vision of how he wanted his own life to be: "It was corny. It was show biz. It was Elvis."[63]

The program was not only an artistic triumph; it was a smash success in every other way. It swamped the competition in the ratings. The press, the TV executives, and Elvis fans alike were ecstatic. The King was back.

The New Music

"If I Can Dream" had been released as a single a few weeks before the show, but afterwards its sales exploded. By January it was number twelve—the biggest Elvis hit since "I'm Yours" in 1965 and his first million seller in three years. The special's soundtrack album also charted high, at number eight.

In the wake of this newfound strength, Elvis wanted to retire from movies to concentrate on recording and live performance. Because of existing contracts, however, he had three more films to complete. These were a western called *Charro!*, a movie about a traveling show called *The Trouble with Girls*, and *Change of Habit*, in which Elvis plays a doctor working in a slum who falls for plainclothes nun Mary Tyler Moore. After these, Presley's only appearances on film would be in performance documentaries.

Presley also started a new phase of intense recording creativity. In January he recorded a new album in Memphis—the first time he had recorded in his hometown since signing with RCA. Legendary

---

Elvis on the Screen

Jerry Hopkins, in Elvis, *quotes others on the way Presley was wasted on bad movies.*

"Many felt Elvis was talented. Even the hard-to-please Bosley Crowther of the *New York Times* had said, 'This boy can act,' about his portrayal in *King Creole*. . . . Others concurred. Don Siegel, the director of *Flaming Star*, said Elvis had switched from [rocker] Little Richard to [acting coach Konstantin] Stanislavsky, had become a Method actor who 'jumps out at you from the screen.' [Actress] Yvonne Craig said she'd seen but one other actor more at ease while doing scenes, Spencer Tracy. Excusing some of his sadder efforts, even [gossip columnist] Hedda Hopper came to Elvis's defense, saying, so what if he wasn't a trained actor, neither was Gary Cooper; he learned on-camera too. . . .

Elvis apparently disagreed in 1963, when he said, 'I've had intellectuals tell me that I've got to progress as an actor, explore new horizons, take on new challenges, all that routine. I'd like to progress. But I'm smart enough to realize that you can't bite off more than you can chew in this racket. You can't go beyond your limitations. They want me to try an artistic picture. That's fine. Maybe I can pull it off someday. But not now. I've done eleven pictures and they've all made money. A certain type of audience likes me. I entertain them with what I'm doing. I'd be a fool to tamper with that kind of success.'"

producer Chips Moman recorded the session. Moman's studio, American Recording, had created hits for such artists as the Box Tops, Dionne Warwick, and Wilson Pickett.

Moman's house band (the resident musicians who backed many of the singers using his studio) was one of the best in the country: guitarist Reggie Young, organist Bobby Emmons, bassist Tommy Cogbill, and drummer Gene Christman. Like Presley, these young musicians were white Southerners who had been deeply influenced by black R&B and gospel. They were, in a sense, carrying on Presley's tradition, continuing the merger between white and black music that Elvis had pioneered.

Presley, Moman, and the band worked together beautifully, and the American Recording sessions represent the most productive single session of Elvis's career. In less than a week, he cut three Top Ten songs ("In the Ghetto," "Suspicious Minds," and "Don't Cry Daddy"), along with a string of other solid tunes like "Long Black Limousine" and "I'm Movin' On." A second session the following month produced another strong batch of songs, including "Kentucky Rain" and "Only the Strong Survive."

Presley also started performing live again on a regular basis. He had been away from the concert stage for almost a decade because Colonel Parker couldn't figure out a way to make live shows as profitable as movies, and Presley's schedule would not have allowed him to do both.

"A Whole Rejuvenation Thing"

In Jerry Hopkins's Elvis, *executive producer Steve Binder and music producer Bones Howe recall the origins of Presley's 1968 "Comeback Special."*

"Binder: 'I felt very, very strongly that the television special was Elvis's moment of truth. If he did [the equivalent of] another M-G-M movie on the special, he would wipe out his career and he would be known only as that phenomenon who came along in the fifties, shook his hips and had a great manager. On the reverse side, if he could do a special and prove he was still number one, he could have a whole rejuvenation thing going.'

Howe: 'We both felt that if we could create an atmosphere of making Elvis feel he's part of the special, that he was creating the special himself—the same way he was organically involved in producing his own records in the old days, before the movies—then we would have a great special. People would really see Elvis Presley, not what the Colonel wanted them to see.'"

A marquee advertises Elvis's presence at the International Hotel in Las Vegas. Presley and his entourage had a two-week engagement at the Vegas hotel.

But the TV special had rekindled Elvis's desire to sing in public. Besides, he pointed out, the movies weren't making as much money as they once had. They had a series of intense arguments, during which the Colonel threatened to quit; at one point, he even stayed up all night figuring out how much money Presley would owe him if they broke up the partnership. In the end, though, Presley got his way. Parker conceded and went about setting up live shows.

Back to Vegas

Rather than an expensive string of one-nighters around the country, the Colonel set up an engagement at the International Hotel in Las Vegas. For doing two shows a night for two weeks, Presley received a million dollars. This was less money than he could have made playing one-nighters, but the expenses were minimal because there was no travel. Also, Parker liked to gamble, and he relished the chance to spend two weeks in Vegas on business.

In early July Presley went to Los Angeles to begin rehearsals. He assembled a crack band: bassist Jerry Scheff, drummer Ronnie Tutt, pianist Larry Muhoberac, guitarist John Wilkinson, and a legendary lead guitarist from Louisiana, James Burton. This basic group was augmented by a full orchestra plus a member of the Memphis Mafia, Charlie Hodge, on acoustic guitar and vocals. In addition, Presley had two vocal teams: a male gospel quartet, the Imperials, and a female group, the Sweet Inspirations (led by Cissy Houston, the mother of Whitney Houston).

Reporters gather around Elvis Presley during a press conference at the International Hotel. Elvis's engagements in Las Vegas brought over a hundred thousand people to the hotel, more than any other performer in history.

Even with his new confidence, Elvis was worried about the gig. He remembered well the disastrous Vegas appearance he had made in 1956, when the crowd at the New Frontier had watched him stonily, and many had walked out. Besides, his performance skills were still rusty, and there was precious little rehearsal time to work out the show's kinks.

He need not have worried. He was a smash success from the opening night. The capacity crowd was roaring its approval before he was even onstage, before he even opened his mouth. The frantic applause and cheering continued—all night, every night. The reviews of this engagement were as ecstatic as the crowd; typical was *Newsweek*'s comment, "There are several incredible things about Elvis, but the most incredible is his staying power in a world where meteoric careers fade like shooting stars."[64]

As the engagement continued, Elvis began to relax. He made jokes and off-hand remarks. He made fun of himself, telling the crowd to ask each other, "Is that him? I thought he was bigger than that."[65] He changed the order of songs frequently, often in midshow, a practice that kept his musicians on their toes. But he always included his current single, "Suspicious Minds," and his traditional closer, "Can't Help Falling in Love."

By the end of the month he had brought in over a hundred thousand people, more than any other Vegas performer to date. Longtime Vegas-watchers were astonished; most people had assumed that a mainstream performer like Barbra Streisand would have better drawing power. But as Glen D. Hardin, the piano player who replaced Larry Muhoberac, remarked, "[W]ith Elvis it was full, full, full. Elvis was the magic word."[66]

When it was over, Presley took a short vacation with Priscilla and some of the Memphis Mafia, and then he went on the road. This set a work pattern for the singer that would continue until his death: Vegas engagements and strings of one-nighters, punctuated by recording and vacations.

Trouble in Paradise

Work was going well, but Elvis's personal life was a long way from perfection. Despite his professional success and luxurious lifestyle, Presley was beginning to have serious problems.

For one thing, fame had increasingly cut him off from reality. He was afraid to go out in public and habitually went to bizarre extremes such as renting entire movie houses all night or arranging for department stores to open so he could go on shopping sprees.

Further cutting him off was the Memphis Mafia, which surrounded him at all times. His old friends continued to indulge his need for comfort, security, constant entertainment, and familiar surroundings.

When Priscilla objected, he justified the Mafia's presence by pointing out that he had been receiving death threats for years.

All this protection, coupled with the ability to indulge his every whim, meant that Presley never grew to maturity. He had been coddled by his mother as a boy. He had been a celebrity since adolescence. And so he missed out on virtually all normal adult activities. He could never go for a walk by himself. He could never go shopping without creating a riot.

He had never once been in a bank: in the early days in Memphis he'd been too poor, and after the money started coming in he had people run such errands for him. He had never even taken a plane ride by himself. He was as isolated and pampered as genuine royalty. As ex-bodyguard Dave Hebler once put it, "He believes he is a law unto himself. . . . Elvis wouldn't know how much a slice of pizza cost in downtown L.A."[67]

Another factor was Presley's increasingly eccentric behavior. His personal habits had always been unusual, but as he

Years of isolation from the public took their toll on Elvis. His fame prohibited him from going out without the protection of the Memphis Mafia and started to disrupt his relationship with Priscilla (right).

grew older they became more extreme. These eccentricities were things no one in his inner circle would admit—at least not until the string of lurid tell-all books about him began appearing toward the very end of his life.

He disliked bathing, and often went days with only minimal hygiene. Because he stayed up all night and slept until midafternoon, the windows of his bedrooms were always covered with aluminum foil. He was subject to sudden mood shifts, and was known to shoot TV sets if he saw something he didn't like. (He had a particular dislike for Robert Goulet, and allegedly shot out any TV on which he happened to see the actor.)

He always ate exactly what he wanted, which tended to be the heavy, fat-laden foods of his childhood: pork chops with brown gravy, fried peanut-butter-and-banana sandwiches, bacon burnt crisp, well-done hamburgers. He kept three cooks on staff at Graceland, usually older Southern women who loved to indulge him.

Also, he was extremely casual with his finances. His spending on friends was legendary: during one Christmas shopping spree, he spent $38,000 on guns and $80,000 on cars. He loved to give away jew-

---

His Last Big Single

Critic Dave Marsh comments, in Elvis, *on the music made by a rejuvenated Presley in the period after his 1968 comeback, in particular the single "Suspicious Minds."*

"The albums that emerged from these sessions, *From Elvis in Memphis* and . . . the *From Memphis to Vegas/From Vegas to Memphis* set, are the first truly adult records of Elvis' career. . . . Very little of what Elvis recorded in Memphis is rock and roll; none of it is straight blues. Yet all of the tracks derive their sense of aggression from rock, and their groove is inevitably born of the blues. . . .

'Suspicious Minds' is the archetype [perfect example] and the apex [top] of all of Elvis' late-Sixties music. It was the last Number One single of his career, and it earned its stature, for it was also by far the most well-crafted single he ever made.

In structure, 'Suspicious Minds' is deceptively simple. Led by a propulsive bass line, the record at first seems to boil down to Elvis and a choir of female voices. But what's really going on is seamless modern record-making. . . . Elvis is not simply working at the peak of his form: he has reached a level of exaltation he hadn't known since the boat left for West Germany."

Elvis shares a happy moment with his family. When his marriage to Priscilla broke up in 1972, Elvis was devastated.

elry so much that he hired a jeweler to travel with him, sample cases at the ready. One time he bought fourteen Cadillacs in a single day, including one for a woman he didn't know but who had just happened by the lot.

Finally, and most seriously, drugs were becoming a real problem for Presley. Elvis hated hard drugs, and he never drank. But in the army he had been introduced to amphetamines, or speed. This drug, which is highly addictive, helped him stay awake on night duty, and he continued to rely on it long after he left the service. He also needed to stay trim despite his eating habits, so in later years he also began to use diet pills, which are also highly addictive.

At first, Elvis's drug use was tolerated by those around him. It was just another part of the music scene, like guitars or girls. By the time drugs became a serious problem for him, severely impairing his health and judgment, no one had the courage to stop him. He was the King, and the King got whatever he wanted.

All these unhealthy influences combined to put Presley's newfound creative energy in jeopardy. Nearly as quickly as he had found his direction again in the wake of the "Comeback Special," he began to lose it in a haze of drugs and erratic behavior. The final blow to Presley's already fragile personality came in early 1972.

Priscilla Leaves

Perhaps the single biggest factor in Elvis's downhill slide was the breakup of his marriage. Priscilla had been unhappy for

Making a Point of Not Trying

Critic Lester Bangs, in an article reprinted in The Elvis Reader, *recalls that at a 1971 concert Presley was both laughable and magnificent.*

"There was Elvis, dressed up in this ridiculous white suit that looked like some studded Arthurian castle, and he was too fat, and the buckle on his belt was as big as your head except that your head is not made of solid gold, and any lesser man would have been the spittin' image of a Neil Diamond damfool in such a getup, but on Elvis it fit. . . .

Literally, every time this man moved any part of his body the slightest centimeter, tens or tens of thousands of people went berserk. Not Sinatra, not Jagger, not the Beatles, nobody you can come up with ever elicited such hysteria among so many. And this after a decade and a half of crappy records, of making a point of not trying."

some time. She hated the boorish, ever-present Memphis Mafia, and she hated Presley's constant travel. She thought he spoiled Lisa Marie terribly by allowing the child to stay up late, eat junk food, and have whatever toy or treat she wanted. Finally, Priscilla was anxious about Elvis's increasingly heavy drug use.

In late 1971, Presley was named in a paternity suit, in which a woman claimed that he was the father of her baby. There had been many such suits over the years, all settled out of court. This was the first to reach an open courtroom. The suit was dismissed when blood tests proved it was false, but the headlines it created exposed Presley's wild party life and added to the growing distance between Elvis and Priscilla.

The couple tried to make the Christmas season as normal as possible. Graceland's house and drive were outlined with thousands of tiny blue lights. Elvis rented a Memphis movie house for entire nights so he and his family could watch Clint Eastwood and James Bond movies. He lavished presents on them. But the mood was strained, and there were rumors—carefully kept from Elvis—that Priscilla was seeing another man.

The day after Christmas, Priscilla took Lisa Marie to California. Early in 1972, she returned and announced that she was leaving Elvis for good. Elvis was stunned; probably because he was so insulated by the Memphis Mafia and disoriented by drugs, he had had little idea that anything was amiss. The final insult was that Priscilla was leaving him for a man he had introduced her to—karate instructor Mike Stone. In February she moved out of their Los Angeles house and filed for divorce.

It was the most serious personal blow Presley had received since his mother's death. He never recovered from it, and instead fell even deeper into his cycle of drugs, parties, and overeating. Still, he kept working. A performance documentary, *Elvis: That's the Way It Is*, had already been filmed; now another documentary, *Elvis on Tour*, was under way. He also maintained a grueling tour schedule—nineteen shows in fifteen days was typical.

But even constant work couldn't keep depression away. For six months after Priscilla left, he refused to let any of his Memphis Mafia buddies bring their wives or girlfriends around him. In a lurid tell-all book published shortly before the singer's death, former bodyguard Red West claimed that Presley tried to hire a hitman to kill Priscilla's new love. Even Presley's choice of material to sing in concert reflected his pain: he began using introspective, melancholy songs like the bittersweet "Separate Ways" and "You Gave Me a Mountain This Time."

Aloha

In January 1973, Elvis appeared in a project the Colonel had dreamed about for years: a live concert broadcast around the world. "Elvis: Aloha from Hawaii by Satellite" was beamed from Honolulu's International Center. To maintain his image—he was, after all, the King—Presley needed increasingly bigger engagements. This worldwide show, a first for the entertainment field, was a good match, both financially and artistically.

Elvis trained hard to get in shape for the massive undertaking. He dieted, exercised, and worked out with Kang Rhee, his Korean-born karate teacher. He also went on a health-food regimen that included protein drinks, mineral water, and vitamin pills. Supplemented by diet pills, this brought his weight, which had begun to balloon, down to a trim 165 pounds.

Elvis works out with his karate instructor to get in shape for his live worldwide concert, "Elvis: Aloha from Hawaii by Satellite," which took place in January 1973.

In star form, Elvis performs during the "Aloha" broadcast. Despite numerous problems before the telecast, the show was a hit and raised $85,000 for a local charity.

There were endless problems with the show. Clothing designer Bill Belew had created a spectacular all-white jumpsuit, but Presley gave away its ruby-encrusted belt to TV actor Jack Lord, the star of *Hawaii Five-O*. Belew had to frantically create a replacement. There were last-minute changes in the set design and song list.

And there were technical problems: the sound system picked up an electrical hum from the lights, but the crew frantically borrowed thick lead sheets from the navy to muffle the distracting sound.

Despite the problems, the program came off brilliantly. Elvis was in fine form, singing twenty-three songs from the past to the present. He was relaxed and in control, leaning down so fans could kiss him and throwing his trademark scarves for them to catch. Behind him, a neon sign blared "WE LOVE ELVIS" in a dozen languages. At the end, he sailed his cape into the cheering audience, made the Hawaiian "no worries" hand sign, and strode confidently off the stage.

The concert was a benefit that raised $85,000 for a local charity, the Kui Lee Cancer Fund. A live broadcast of the show was transmitted to Asia; as the climax of Elvis Presley Week in Japan, it smashed all previous TV records with an amazing 98 percent audience share. A taped version was later broadcast across Europe and America. It was seen by an estimated 1.5 billion people—the largest single audience to date.

The "Aloha" broadcast was another triumph. But Presley was tired, depressed, and grieving for his lost family. He had been the biggest superstar of all for many years now, and it was an increasingly difficult burden. The end was drawing near.

9 "Elvis Has Left the Building"

The King is dead.

John Lennon after
Presley's death

It's like someone just told me there aren't going to be any more cheeseburgers in the world.

Felton Jarvis, Elvis's producer, on
hearing of Presley's death

In a sense, it's true that Elvis died not blameless but friendless. If you're looking for a tragedy, there it is.

writer Dave Marsh

Elvis was deeply depressed, and no amount of pills or amusement seemed to help. There is no single reason why Presley slid so badly after the burst of creativity that followed his 1968 comeback. Perhaps his divorce, combined with his tendency toward poor health and the intense emotional pressure of simply *being* Elvis Presley, was the final blow.

Things grew especially bleak when Priscilla tried to deny him custody or visitation rights for Lisa Marie. The matter of custody was resolved after Priscilla filed a claim that she had been defrauded during the divorce. She said Presley's attorneys had talked her into accepting an unfair settlement: $1,500 a month and $100,000 in cash.

The new settlement gave her $8,200 a month, half of the money from the California home, stock in Presley's publishing companies, and nearly a million and a half in cash. In return, Elvis got joint custody of Lisa Marie. He told his friends that he had actually gained from the new settlement; for him, a guarantee of seeing his daughter was more important than money.

Meanwhile, Presley was denying he had a drug problem. He considered marijuana, LSD, and hard drugs to be dangerous and stayed away from these substances all his life. But the prescription drugs he used came from doctors, so how could they be bad? One of the few people brave enough to confront the singer about his drug habit was his karate teacher, Kang Rhee. Presley told him that it was the Beatles, who had publicly admitted using marijuana and LSD, who had the drug problem—not Elvis himself.

At one point Presley's West Coast attorney, Ed Hookstratton, hired a private eye to find the source of Elvis's drugs. Hookstratton found that several doctors around the country were writing prescriptions for Elvis or for Mafia members, who turned the drugs over to Presley. Individually, the prescriptions were not illegal, but together they yielded a number of pills far in excess of the legal limit for a single person. Hookstratton later said that he reported this activity to federal and state authorities, but that they took no notice.

More Recording, More Gigs

In July 1973, Elvis spent a week recording at the legendary Stax Studios in Memphis. It had been sixteen months since he'd been in a studio. Like American Studios, the site of his 1969 sessions, Stax was responsible for a long string of R&B hits: such artists as Otis Redding, Booker T. and the MGs, and Sam and Dave had recorded memorable music at Stax.

Many of the band members had worked with Elvis on the American sessions. Presley had become increasingly sloppy in the studio, and he did little preparation this time.

Instead, he listened to a stack of demo records until he found one he liked. Once he had decided on a tune, he worked on it casually with the band. Often, he insisted on using the same basic arrangement heard on the demo. In the early days, he had worked endlessly to find an original style and make a song uniquely his. Now, however, he seemed content to record just his famous voice over a basic track.

Elvis recorded only a few tunes each day. He appeared tired and dispirited. Drummer Jerry Carrigan recalled Elvis's shocking appearance: "He was just visibly miserable. And he did something I never saw him do before. He wore the same clothes two days in a row. Normally, his valet would bring clothes and he'd change during the course of the evening."[68]

For several days in a row that the studio was booked, Presley didn't show up at all; the musicians were told that he was sick. Later that year he went back to Stax, but the results were disappointing. The bittersweet ballads from these sessions, like "Help Me" and "Goodtime Charlie's Got the Blues," best reflected the singer's sad mood.

That summer, however, he drew a hundred thousand people to the Vegas Hilton in one month. He was paid more than any other Vegas entertainer to date, plus numerous "incidentals," such as suites for his entire entourage. He was sometimes still plagued by fears that no one would turn out to see him, but as usual the fears were unfounded. Former Presley bodyguard Red West once remarked that it was really up to the Colonel, anyway: "The Colonel made the big decisions [about appearances] and he wasn't wrong."[69]

Detox?

In October 1973, in Santa Monica Superior Court, Elvis and Priscilla were officially divorced. They emerged from the courthouse arm in arm, kissed for the photographers, and parted. Six days later, back in Memphis, Elvis checked into Baptist Memorial for what a spokesman called pneumonia. There has been speculation that the true purpose of his visit was to detoxify himself from the painkiller Demerol.

Presley's eighteen days there were his first prolonged visit to a hospital. Newsmen camped out around the clock, tens of thousands of get-well cards piled up in the hospital hallways, and the singer received so many flowers that he was able to give a bouquet to every patient in the hospital. He installed 24-hour guards, had forbidden food like cheeseburgers smuggled in, and arranged for Linda Thompson, the latest girlfriend to replace Priscilla, to stay with him.

When not in the hospital, Presley's actions were increasingly strange. Once, out of boredom, he fired a pistol at a light switch and missed Linda by inches. On a whim, he flew to Washington, D.C., and showed up unannounced at the White House. He demanded, successfully, to meet President Nixon and received from him a federal drug agent badge. He treated his musicians terribly, insulting them onstage or stranding them at airports, then buying them luxury cars or jewelry the next day.

Other problems besides health and erratic behavior were nagging Presley. One was a six-million-dollar lawsuit against Presley and his bodyguards, in which a man claimed he had been beaten by the Memphis Mafia and that Elvis had not tried to stop them. According to the lawsuit, the plaintiff had paid a Mafia member to let him into a party at Elvis's hotel suite in Lake Tahoe, Nevada. The Mafia member, however, left the would-be guest stranded in the hotel hallway, where he threw some switches that turned off the electricity to Presley's suite. Three Mafia members came out, the man said, and beat him up while Presley looked on.

The case created huge legal fees; worse, it forced Presley and Parker to make their finances public for the first

President Richard Nixon poses for a photograph with Elvis Presley. The two men met when Presley flew to the White House on a whim.

time. Court documents revealed that Elvis earned $7.25 million in 1974, mostly from touring. After taxes and expenses, he had a personal net income that year of about $1.5 million but a deficit of $700,000. In other words, Presley had spent much more than he had made—not on business expenses but on himself.

Also, as Presley neared his fortieth birthday, attacks in the press began to appear. Critics said that his shows were sloppy, and that he was lazy because he knew his fans would follow him anyway. *Los Angeles Times* rock critic Robert Hilburn, once a devoted fan, wrote, "Maybe it's time for Elvis to retire. . . . At

---

An Enormous Appetite

Jane and Michael Stern, in Elvis World, *comment on the many tales of Elvis's eating extravagance.*

"Elvis . . . if you believe what you read, ate more food than any other man who ever lived.

Take bacon. Elvis liked bacon, burnt to a crisp. Four pounds at a time, in a bowl for snacking, on top of the piano, accompanied by two large pizzas with the works. He liked cheeseburgers and could down a dozen at a time, topping off the meal with a gallon of ice cream. His dressing room at Paramount needed two refrigerator-freezers, one stocked exclusively with ice cream. He easily ingested fifteen tacos at a single sitting. He put so much pepper on his eggs they turned black and ate so many Spanish omelets that he created an egg shortage in Tennessee. Thirty cups of yogurt, eight massive honeydew melons, a hundred dollars' worth of ice cream bars: all gone in a night's eating binge. When he was on a diet, he confined himself to sausage biscuits, six or seven of them at a shot, sopped in a half pound of melted butter.

All of the above statistics are given as fact by Elvis' biographers. No doubt, the man had a healthy appetite; he always did; and in the final years, his metabolism slowed and trapped him. But what's wonderful about the preposterous accounts of his binges is that in the telling they become an everyday Elvis feat. If Elvis ever did anything once—and if anyone saw him do it—it was then written (in its most lurid and exaggerated form) as part of the superhuman Elvis Legend."

40, his records are increasingly uneven, his choice of material sometimes ludicrous, and his concert performances often sloppy. Worst of all, there is no purpose or personal vision in his music anymore."[70]

His fans did follow him, regardless. Birthday greetings poured in at the rate of six hundred a day. Two thousand visitors came by Graceland on January 8, 1975, and radio stations all across the world celebrated the King's fortieth birthday by playing his records all day.

The Last Years

In his final years Presley alternated work with hospitalization. His ailments ranged from an enlarged colon and hypertension to liver, kidney, and eye problems. His drug abuse and eating habits may not have caused these problems, but they certainly aggravated them. In addition, he had a weak heart—a condition he shared with several family members, including his mother.

Although Presley continued to be fascinated with guns and karate, he also became increasingly interested in spiritual matters. Elvis had always been deeply religious, but now his curiosity went beyond traditional Christianity. His hairdresser, Larry Geller, practiced meditation and followed a guru named Paramahansa Yogananda; Presley briefly joined Yogananda's organization as well. His interest in spirituality extended to such areas as astrology, astral traveling, UFOs, and numerology.

Elvis also continued to see a variety of women, often introduced to him by the Memphis Mafia. To hear the Mafia tell it, they took care of all Presley's needs by now and virtually kept him alive from day to day. Dave Hebler once said, "Sometimes, you think you are looking after a child."[71] The singer was often surprisingly kind and gentle with the women. He would read the Bible out loud, and they would cuddle and talk for hours. There were rumors that Presley was too sick for anything more strenuous.

RCA was desperate to have Elvis record again, but he refused to go into a studio. In early 1976 RCA decided to bring recording equipment to him, and Graceland's den became a makeshift studio. After equipment had been installed and musicians brought from Los Angeles and Nashville, however, it was days before Presley agreed to come downstairs. When he did, it was only to record a dozen lackluster tunes. At first Elvis liked recording at home so well that he wanted to do it permanently. A few days later, however, he decided he hated the playback monitors and aimed a shotgun at them; his musicians got the gun away before he could fire.

A year later, a studio was again set up in Graceland. The musicians assembled and waited for days while Elvis found excuses not to record. There were rumors that he was off on a one-man vigilante mission, avenging himself on the drug dealers who had addicted a relative to heroin. But the real reason was probably anger and depression that three bodyguards he had fired for rough conduct (including the hallway beating incident) were about to come out with a tell-all book, *Elvis: What Happened?* Guitarist John Wilkinson recalled, "He said he loved them like brothers and he couldn't understand why they'd want to stab him in the back."[72]

By this time, Presley's live shows were disasters. The drugs were beginning to

Near the end of his life, Elvis's live shows were catastrophes. His heavy drug use severely impaired his health and judgment, causing him to forget lyrics, ramble incoherently, and miss performances.

ton Rouge, Louisiana, he did not leave his hotel room and never made it to the auditorium.

In June 1977, Elvis played his final show, in Indianapolis, Indiana. By all accounts, it was not a bad show—at least not as bad as some others. Presley joked with the audience and was in good voice. It ended with his usual closing tune, "Can't Help Falling in Love." Then came another traditional element of an Elvis show, an announcement designed to discourage fans from trying to get backstage: "Ladies and gentlemen, Elvis has left the building."

"It's Over. He's Gone"

Later in the summer of 1977, Lisa Marie, now nine, arrived for a few weeks' visit— the longest time she had spent at Graceland since the divorce. Elvis's last days were spent playing with her, talking on the phone, entertaining guests, reading spiritual books, playing racquetball, and watching TV. On August 14 he started a fast in preparation for a new tour. Lisa Marie was due to go back to California in two days, and the tour was scheduled to begin on the following day.

On August 15, Elvis and his current girlfriend, Ginger Alden, made a late-night visit to a dentist, and Elvis had two teeth filled. By 2:30 the next morning, he was playing racquetball with Ginger and two friends. About 4 A.M., everyone went to bed. Ginger claimed later that she and Elvis had talked about wedding plans.

Ginger eventually fell asleep, but Elvis read in bed. Later that morning Elvis's aunt delivered the morning paper to him, along with a glass of water. Presley told her that he was going to sleep soon and would

seriously affect his stage presence. He dropped the mike, forgot lyrics, rambled incoherently, and was often helped offstage by bodyguards. At one show in Ba-

awaken at 7:00 that night to get ready for the tour. At 9:00 A.M. Ginger woke up briefly. Elvis was still reading; he said he was going into the bathroom to read more, and Ginger went back to sleep.

Sometime between 1:00 and 2:00 P.M., August 16, Ginger awoke and found Elvis slumped on the bathroom floor. He had suffered a heart attack while sitting in an armchair, reading a book called *The Scientific Search for the Face of Jesus.* Panicked, Ginger called downstairs. Mafia members Joe Esposito and Al Strada ran upstairs and rolled Presley over; he was not breathing. Strada called a doctor, Esposito tried to revive Elvis, and Vernon and Lisa Marie came rushing in. Ginger tried to push the little girl away, but she ran to the bathroom's other door and saw her father on the floor.

Dr. George Nichopolous, Elvis's doctor, arrived at the same time as the ambulance. "Dr. Nick," as he was known, accompanied Esposito and Elvis's step-brother, Dave

Ginger Alden stands beside a painting of her late boyfriend, Elvis Presley. Alden found Elvis slumped on the bathroom floor after suffering a heart attack on August 16, 1977.

Stanley, in the ambulance to Baptist Memorial. Everyone else went into Grandma Minnie Mae's room to pray.

Resuscitation attempts continued en route, and at the hospital a trauma team worked to revive the famous patient. But it was no use. Hospital vice president Maurice Elliott recalled, "They worked on him for about thirty minutes and then Dr. Nick came in, his head down. He said, 'It's over. He's gone.' You could see tears come to his eyes and everybody there started crying."[73]

"Have You Heard the News?"

Newsmen had been swarming around the hospital even before Elvis arrived, having gotten word on the emergency radio frequency. But the official news of Presley's death was not given until Dr. Nick could inform the family at Graceland and Esposito could reach the Colonel, who was in Maine, ready for the start of the tour. Minutes later, the world learned that the King was dead.

An autopsy was performed to determine the cause of death. That evening, coroner Jerry Francisco and Elvis's physician held a press conference to announce that Presley's death was due to an erratic heartbeat brought on by severe cardiovascular (heart) disease.

Prompted by the recently published book by the fired bodyguards, reporters asked about Elvis's use of drugs. Francisco denied any indication of drug abuse. The only drugs found in Presley's body, he said, were those prescribed by his physician for long-standing hypertension and colon problems. However, a final

Headlines from Memphis's local newspaper, the Commercial Appeal, *announced the death of Elvis Presley on August 17, 1977.*

medical report released later reported traces of ten prescription drugs in Presley's system.

Polypharmacy, the increased effect of several drugs acting together, may have been a factor in Presley's death. Dr. Nichopoulos was later investigated, following allegations of malpractice; the charges included stories of illegal prescriptions for more than five thousand pills just in the last seven months of Presley's life. The investigation found minor problems such as inadequate record keeping, but "Dr. Nick" was eventually cleared of all major charges.

The Viewing

Less than an hour after Presley's death was announced, on August 16, 1977, a crowd had formed outside Graceland. Dozens of people had portable radios tuned to stations broadcasting Elvis records and news bulletins about him. The huge crowd—estimated at eighty thousand at its peak—kept up a vigil for days.

Reporters from all around the world flew in, and every television network scheduled instant specials. The *National Enquirer* tabloid alone assigned twenty reporters to the story. All over Memphis, anyone who had known Elvis even slightly was interviewed. All the flowers in town, meanwhile, were at Graceland—over three thousand floral arrangements—and every florist ran out. An estimated five tons of flowers had to be brought in from other cities to fill the orders.

Midday on August 17, the enormous crowd watched as a white hearse, accompanied by a caravan of police motorcycles, brought Elvis's body from the Memphis Funeral Home to Graceland. After a private service, the public was allowed in.

Deep Sadness

In Jerry Hopkins's Elvis: The Final Years, *country singer T. G. Sheppard, a friend of Presley's, comments on Elvis's downward spiral following the divorce.*

"I saw so many hours of sadness and hurt and bewilderment, as to life in general, as to maybe what was happening to him. When the marriage failed, it was such a damaging blow. Here's a man who was brought up in a southern, Christian environment, where marriage was labeled forever. It was very special. You got married, you had kids and you grew old together. Divorce didn't happen. Marriage was very sacred. I think when that failed, it was a turning point in his life. Things seemed to change. It never was the same. The health problems came, the problems that didn't seem to appear before. Seemed like life became more difficult. It didn't flow like it did before."

The line stretched for miles, and dozens fainted in the 90-degree heat. Some may have collapsed on purpose, because then it was guaranteed they could go inside the gates for treatment at a medical tent. Along the street, entrepreneurs were selling memorial T-shirts and lapel buttons printed up overnight. At one point, tragedy struck again when a drunk driver plowed into the mourners; two were killed and a third critically injured.

Through all this, Elvis lay inside a nine-hundred-pound copper-lined coffin beneath a crystal chandelier. He wore a white suit, a light blue shirt, and a white tie.

Tributes from singers and celebrities came flooding in. "We lost a good friend," Frank Sinatra said. "There's no way to measure the impact he made on society or the void that he leaves," said singer Pat Boone. President Jimmy Carter said that Elvis's death "deprives our country of a

Droves of mourning fans pour through the gates of Graceland, eager to pay their respects during the public viewing on August 17.

*Fans congregate along Elvis Presley Boulevard to watch as the funeral
procession transports Elvis's body to a nearby cemetery.*

part of itself," and that his music and personality "permanently changed the face of American popular culture." [74]

Some reactions to Presley's passing were less reverent. Writer Nick Tosches recalls seeing a sign outside a Baptist church in Orangeburg, South Carolina, just days after his death, that said: "All That Hip Shaking Killed Elvis." [75] And Big Mama Thornton, the blues singer who recorded the original version of "Hound Dog," was asked by reporters how she felt about receiving only $100 for it while Presley made millions. Her response was a sad reflection on Elvis's fate: "I'm still here to *spend* my hundred dollars." [76]

Presley's memorial service featured some of the world's finest gospel singers.

Kathy Westmoreland, one of Elvis's backup singers, performed "My Heavenly Father Watches Over Me." Jake Hess, who had been such a huge influence on Presley as part of the Statesmen Quartet, sang "Known Only to Him." James Blackwood sang "How Great Thou Art." The Stamps, who had often backed Presley, performed "His Hand in Mine" and "Sweet, Sweet Spirit."

In a private ceremony, Elvis was buried in a white marble mausoleum in a nearby cemetery. Later, following a bizarre attempt to steal the body from the cemetery, Vernon moved the coffin to the Meditation Garden in Graceland. Elvis rests there today, alongside the bodies of his mother and his grandmother.

Elvis Lives!

Elvis is a riddle that cannot be solved, but he gives us a great deal to think about and a lot of great music to listen to while we're thinking.

writer Kevin Quain

He was an integrator. Elvis was a blessing. They wouldn't let black music through. He opened the door for black music.

singer Little Richard

He taught white America to get down.

singer James Brown

As a young man, Elvis Presley rocked the world and influenced a generation of performers. As an adult, he was both a legend and a has-been. Dead, he is even more famous (and profitable) than when he was alive. Elvis was once a living legend; now he is a myth.

There are dozens of theories about Elvis's death, including speculation that Presley faked his own demise and is living quietly under an assumed name. There have been hundreds of postdeath Elvis sightings—in shopping malls, at burger joints, even guiding the space shuttle. Such incidents indicate the passionate feelings Presley arouses. Some fans simply refuse to believe that he is dead.

But Presley does live on in more concrete ways. His grave is the focal point of Graceland, which is the second-most-

Elvismania

Critic Richard Corliss, in a Time *article written shortly after Presley's death and reprinted in* The Elvis Reader, *comments on the singer's unique status.*

"Elvismania transcends the usual devotion to a white-hot celebrity, even one who has died before his time. Rudolph Valentino, Will Rogers, James Dean and Marilyn Monroe may have left indelible niches in the hearts of their fans, but few built shrines to them. Rumors of their survival rarely blossomed into testimony of posthumous [after death] visitations. Nor did their homes become cathedral theme parks."

visited home in America (after the White House). The mansion, at 3764 Elvis Presley Boulevard, is listed on the National Register of Historic Places and receives seven hundred thousand visitors a year. It is the centerpiece of a thriving business community in Memphis that specializes in keeping Presley's name alive. There are Elvis tours, Elvis hotels, Elvis taxis, Elvis museums, and more Elvis tours.

Elvismania is by no means limited to Memphis. Hundreds of entertainers around the world, professional and amateur, impersonate the singer. Dozens of conventions pack in fans yearly. In Japan, one fan club has published a complete account of every concert Elvis gave between 1970 and 1977—all 1,126 performances, with complete data for each on attendance, location, time, date, which jumpsuit he wore and which scarf, belt, and buckle went with it.

Books about Elvis are also big business. More arrive every year: tell-all hatchet jobs by former employees, fond recollections by family or people who knew him, cookbooks detailing his favorite foods, and more. Millions of pieces of Elvis memorabilia, authorized and bootleg, are manufactured every year—everything from life-size Elvis dolls that perspire and guitar-shaped hairbrushes to Elvis wines and Elvis bottles of bourbon (named, ironically, for a man who never drank).

Elvis World

In Elvis World, *their book celebrating the Presley legend, Jane and Michael Stern try to analyze the phenomenon itself.*

"Elvis World is not one place. It is the universe defined by all he stands for: music, of course, and movies, but also the cascade of material things he consumed, the fans he enraptured and stuffed shirts he outraged. . . .

Gossip mongers relish Elvis. But tabloid slander is not the true road into Elvis World. To get mired in the dirt is to miss the exaltation. Whatever his health problems, they were scrupulously kept private when he was alive. And now that he is dead, they are nothing more than a banal [dull] footnote to a career that was extraordinary in every other way. . . .

There was a time when he was merely the most popular entertainer in history. He is more than that now. He is a symbol of America as recognizable as the flag. Show his picture to a taxi driver in Thailand or a housewife in Tasmania or a ten-year-old child in Bangor, Maine, and they will all recognize him. While working on this book, we never once met anyone who asked, 'Elvis who?'"

The U.S. Postal Service issued an Elvis Presley stamp in 1992—the first stamp in the history of the postal service to honor a rock musician.

Several people around the world have legally changed their names to Elvis Presley; rock star Declan McManus is better known to his fans as Elvis Costello. In 1992 the U.S. Postal Service issued a hugely popular Elvis stamp—the first to honor a rock musician—following a contest to decide which picture (a young, thin Elvis or an older, heavier Elvis) should be used.

But all the Elvismania in the world cannot hide a simple truth: Elvis Presley was a *musician*. As an artist and an entertainer, he changed American popular music forever. He shook the music scene out of its bland indifference and paved the way for the giddy, raw power of the rock revolution.

He also did more than anyone to take the passion, intensity, dignity, and rich emotion of black popular music outside the community that invented it. Some critics complain that he exploited black culture, taking something away without giving enough back. But it can also be argued that he bravely bridged a wide racial gap; by fusing black and white styles and presenting the new mix to a mainstream audience, Presley helped bring diversity to the music world.

One thing remains: Elvis Presley was the King of Rock and Roll.

Notes

Chapter 1: The Early Years

1. Howard A. DeWitt, *Elvis: The Sun Years*. Ann Arbor, MI: Popular Culture, Ink, 1993, p. 46.
2. Quoted in Jerry Hopkins, *Elvis*. New York: Simon & Schuster, 1971, p. 22.
3. Quoted in DeWitt, *Elvis: The Sun Years*, p. 58.
4. Quoted in DeWitt, *Elvis: The Sun Years*, p. 44.
5. Quoted in Hopkins, *Elvis*, p. 22.
6. Dave Marsh, *Elvis*. New York: Thunder's Mouth Press, 1992, p. 9.
7. Quoted in Marsh, *Elvis*, p. 9.
8. Quoted in Peter Guralnick, *Last Train to Memphis: The Rise of Elvis Presley*. Boston: Little, Brown, 1994, p. 26.
9. Quoted in Hopkins, *Elvis*, p. 32.
10. Quoted in Guralnick, *Last Train to Memphis*, p. 35.
11. DeWitt, *Elvis: The Sun Years*, p. 78.
12. DeWitt, *Elvis: The Sun Years*, p. 81.

Chapter 2: The First Recordings

13. Quoted in Hopkins, *Elvis*, p. 68.
14. Quoted in Hopkins, *Elvis*, p. 65.
15. Quoted in Marsh, *Elvis*, p. 22.
16. Quoted in Marsh, *Elvis*, p. 21.
17. Quoted in Marsh, *Elvis*, p. 23.
18. Marsh, *Elvis*, p. 23.
19. Quoted in Guralnick, *Last Train to Memphis*, p. 90.
20. Quoted in Marsh, *Elvis*, p. 23.
21. Quoted in Hopkins, *Elvis*, p. 71.
22. DeWitt, *Elvis: The Sun Years*, p. 144.
23. Quoted in Guralnick, *Last Train to Memphis*, p. 92.
24. Quoted in Guralnick, *Last Train to Memphis*, p. 92.

Chapter 3: The Rise to Fame

25. Quoted in DeWitt, *Elvis: The Sun Years*, p. 149.
26. Marsh, *Elvis*, p. 54.
27. Quoted in DeWitt, *Elvis: The Sun Years*, p. 154.
28. Quoted in Guralnick, *Last Train to Memphis*, pp. 132–33.
29. Marsh, *Elvis*, p. 58.
30. Guralnick, *Last Train to Memphis*, p. 190.
31. Marsh, *Elvis*, p. 63.

Chapter 4: The Big Time

32. Quoted in DeWitt, *Elvis: The Sun Years*, p. 239.
33. DeWitt, *Elvis: The Sun Years*, p. 239.
34. Quoted in Hopkins, *Elvis*, p. 309.
35. Quoted in Hopkins, *Elvis*, p. 152.
36. Guralnick, *Last Train to Memphis*, p. 245.
37. Quoted in Guralnick, *Last Train to Memphis*, p. 298.
38. Quoted in Guralnick, *Last Train to Memphis*, p. 277.
39. Quoted in Marsh, *Elvis*, p. 106.

Chapter 5: The Early Movies

40. Quoted in Guralnick, *Last Train to Memphis*, p. 323.
41. Quoted in Guralnick, *Last Train to Memphis*, p. 406.
42. Quoted in Guralnick, *Last Train to Memphis*, p. 426.
43. Quoted in Hopkins, *Elvis*, p. 191.
44. Quoted in Guralnick, *Last Train to Memphis*, p. 434.

Chapter 6: The Army Years

45. Quoted in Hopkins, *Elvis*, p. 207.
46. Quoted in Guralnick, *Last Train to Memphis*, 469.
47. Quoted in Hopkins, *Elvis*, p. 213.
48. Quoted in Guralnick, *Last Train to Memphis*, p. 474.
49. Quoted in Guralnick, *Last Train to Memphis*, p. 488.
50. Quoted in Hopkins, *Elvis*, p. 235.

Chapter 7: The Movie Years

51. Quoted in Hopkins, *Elvis*, p. 247.
52. Quoted in Hopkins, *Elvis*, p. 247.
53. Quoted in Hopkins, *Elvis*, p. 253
54. Quoted in Hopkins, *Elvis*, p. 325
55. Quoted in Hopkins, *Elvis*, p. 292.
56. Quoted in Hopkins, *Elvis*, p. 327.
57. Quoted in Hopkins, *Elvis*, p. 175.
58. Marsh, *Elvis*, p. 156.

Chapter 8: Comeback

59. Marsh, *Elvis*, p. 163.
60. Marsh, *Elvis*, pp. 175–6.
61. Quoted in Hopkins, *Elvis*, p. 345.
62. Marsh, *Elvis*, p. 176.

63. Marsh, *Elvis*, p. 181.
64. Quoted in Hopkins, *Elvis*, p. 376.
65. Quoted in Hopkins, *Elvis*, p. 372.
66. Quoted in Hopkins, *Elvis*, p. 368.
67. Quoted in Steve Dunleavy, *Elvis: What Happened?* New York: Ballantine Books, 1977, p. 86.

Chapter 9: "Elvis Has Left the Building"

68. Quoted in Jerry Hopkins, *Elvis: The Final Years*. New York: St. Martin's Press, 1980, p. 107.
69. Quoted in Dunleavy, *Elvis*, p. 288.
70. Quoted in Hopkins, *Elvis: The Final Years*, p. 138.
71. Quoted in Dunleavy, *Elvis*, p. 202.
72. Quoted in Hopkins, *Elvis: The Final Years*, p. 208.
73. Quoted in Hopkins, *Elvis: The Final Years*, p. 239.
74. Quoted in Hopkins, *Elvis: The Final Years*, p. 245.
75. Quoted in Kevin Quain, *The Elvis Reader: Texts and Sources on the King of Rock 'n' Roll*. New York: St. Martin's, 1992, p. 273.
76. Quoted in Quain, *The Elvis Reader*, p. 73.

For Further Reading

Mick Farren (editor/compiler), *Elvis in His Own Words*. London: Omnibus, 1977. A collection of quotes by Presley. No sources or dates are given, but the quotes are still entertaining and enlightening.

Tony Gentry, *Elvis Presley*. New York: Chelsea House, 1994.

Jerry Hopkins, *Elvis*. New York: Simon & Schuster, 1971. A somewhat dull but straightforward biography that covers the basic facts of Elvis's life through the late 1960s.

———, *Elvis: The Final Years*. New York: St. Martin's Press, 1980. A sequel to the author's 1971 book, covering Presley's last years. Marred (as is the earlier book) by a lack of citations or index.

Dave Marsh, *Elvis*. New York: Thunder's Mouth Press, 1992. (Originally published in 1982 by Straight Arrow Books.) An intelligent, fair, and passionate book by a rock critic. Not a full biography, but an extended essay with excellent graphics.

David Rubel, *Elvis Presley: The Rise of Rock and Roll*. Brookfield, CT: Millbrook Press, 1991.

Additional Works Consulted

Books

Howard A. DeWitt, *Elvis: The Sun Years.* Ann Arbor, MI: Popular Culture, Ink, 1993. A thoroughly researched look at Presley's early recording years by a university history professor.

Elaine Dundy, *Elvis and Gladys.* New York: Macmillan, 1985. Focuses on the close relationship between Presley and his mother.

Steve Dunleavy with Red West, Sonny West, and Dave Hebler, *Elvis: What Happened?* New York: Ballantine Books, 1977. A tell-all book. Ghostwriter Dunleavy records the reminiscences of three disgruntled former Presley employees.

Albert Goldman, *Elvis.* New York: McGraw-Hill, 1981. The most hyped of all Elvis biographies, and the worst—vicious, lurid, and elitist. Based on stories told by a disgruntled Presley bodyguard.

Peter Guralnick, *Last Train to Memphis: The Rise of Elvis Presley.* Boston: Little, Brown, 1994. Easily the best book ever written about Elvis Presley. Wide ranging, detailed, respectful, and perceptive. This book takes the story as far as Elvis's induction into the army; Guralnick, a distinguished expert on American music, is working on the second volume.

Ted Harrison, *Elvis People: The Cult of the King.* London: Fount, 1992. An examination by a British writer of Elvis as a postdeath religious phenomenon.

Greil Marcus, *Dead Elvis.* Garden City, NY: Doubleday, 1991. A look by a rock critic at the ways in which Elvis lives on after death. Arty and pretentious, but with some valuable insights.

———, *Mystery Train: Images of America in Rock 'n' Roll Music.* New York: Dutton, 1976. The last essay in this book, "Elvis: Presliad," is a long meditation on what Elvis might have achieved if he had not connected with Colonel Parker. As pretentious as Marcus's other book, but with a few good insights.

Elizabeth McKeon, Ralph Gevirta, and Julie Bandy, *Fit for a King: The Elvis Presley Cookbook.* Nashville: Rutledge Hill Press, 1992. Recipes for Elvis's favorite foods and other typical Southern dishes.

Patricia Jobe Pierce, *The Ultimate Elvis: Elvis Presley Day by Day.* New York: Simon & Schuster, 1994. For diehard fanatics only: a day-by-day "diary" of every day in Presley's life, plus trivia lists, biographies of important people in Elvis's life, and more.

Priscilla Beaulieu Presley, *Elvis and Me.* New York: G. P. Putnam's, 1985. A sugar-coated memoir by Elvis's ex-wife, who is the mother of Lisa Marie Presley, his only heir.

Kevin Quain, *The Elvis Reader: Texts and Sources on the King of Rock 'n' Roll.* New York: St. Martin's, 1992. A collection of fiction and nonfiction from the 1950s to the present. The sources are as diverse as rocker Mojo Nixon, writer

Roy Blount Jr., musicologist Richard Middleton, and novelist Don DeLillo.

Michael and Jane Stern, *Elvis World*. New York: Knopf, 1987. An affectionate look at how the Elvis legend has shaped American pop culture. Not serious history, but it does capture the tacky, good-natured humor that was a big part of Elvis and his mystique. Terrific graphics.

Dirk Vellenga, *Elvis and the Colonel*. New York: Delacorte, 1988. A book by a Dutch journalist detailing Parker's origins and relationship with Elvis.

Steven Zmijewsky and Boris Zmijewsky, *Elvis: The Films and Career of Elvis Presley*. Secaucus, NJ: Citadel Press, 1976. A guide to the feature films and some of the documentaries, with cast lists, release dates, and brief descriptions of each film.

Videos

Steve Binder (director), *Elvis: '68 Comeback Special*. Los Angeles: Media Home Entertainment, 1985. A video version of Presley's triumphant return to live performance. The staged dance sequences have aged poorly, but Elvis is magnificent.

Patrick Michael Murphy (producer), *Elvis: The Lost Performances*. Culver City, CA: MGM/UA Home Entertainment and Turner Entertainment, 1992. Interesting outtakes from two Elvis documentaries filmed in the early 1970s, "lost" in a warehouse for nearly twenty years.

Denis Sanders (director), *Elvis: That's The Way It Is*. New York: MGM/UA Home Video, 1972. Well-made documentary on the preparations leading up to a 1970 Presley engagement in Las Vegas, with extensive rehearsal and concert footage.

Andrew Solt (writer, director), *Elvis: The Great Performances*. Burbank, CA: Buena Vista Video and Andrew Solt Productions, 1990. An excellent compilation of Elvis in musical performance. Includes early TV appearances, movie clips, and an intense performance filmed only weeks before his death.

Andrew Solt and Malcolm Leo (writers, producers, directors), *This Is Elvis*. Burbank, CA: Warner Brothers Video, 1981. A semidocumentary film tracing Elvis's life. The re-created "docudrama" portions are cheesy, and the historical clips can be found on Solt's other documentary films.

Index

Picture Credits

Cover photo: Archive Photos

AP/Wide World Photos, 11, 13 (top), 18, 32, 39, 61, 64, 66, 88, 94, 95, 97, 98, 101

Archive Photos, 9, 15, 16, 41, 42, 60 (bottom), 70, 81, 83, 87, 96

The Bettmann Archive, 26, 30, 59, 63

Photofest, 57, 71, 74, 85, 91

Springer/Bettmann Film Archive, 54

Stock Montage, Inc., 43

UPI/Bettmann, 13 (bottom), 20, 28, 37, 45, 49, 51, 52, 53, 60 (top), 68, 73, 78, 82

About the Author

Adam Woog, the author of several books for young people and adults, lives in Seattle, Washington, with his wife and daughter. For Lucent Books, he has written *The United Nations, Poltergeists, The Importance of Harry Houdini, The Importance of Louis Armstrong, The Importance of Duke Ellington,* and *The Mysterious Death of Amelia Earhart.* He voted for the young Elvis stamp.